# Endings. Beginnings . . .

## WHEN MIDLIFE WOMEN
## LEAVE HOME
## IN SEARCH OF AUTHENTICITY

Ani Liggett, Ph.D.

*For Rose ~*
*Enjoy!*
*Ani Liggett*

Published by BeMe Press
Lafayette, CO


Cover photo © 2009 by Sheila Durkin Dierks
Cover and book design © 2009 by Vicki McVey


ISBN 978-0-9842227-0-4
LCCN 2009909761

"Love after Love" from COLLECTED POEMS 1948-1984
by Derek Walcott. Copyright 1986 by Derek Walcott.
Reprinted by permission of Farrar, Straus and Giroux,
LLC.

# DEDICATION

To the courageous and generous women
who shared their stories with me

# TABLE OF CONTENTS

# Preface

This book was born one summer afternoon as I was in the throes of my own midlife transition—having moved across the country in response (once again) to my heart's call to a more authentic life. It was a Sunday afternoon and I was lying in a hammock under a fragrant blossoming tree reading William Bridges's book *Transitions*. I have long been interested in the dynamics of change and transition, human or otherwise. As I thought deeply about endings and beginnings and about the perils of the empty in-between space, I realized that for women the transition journey is more complex than the mythical hero's journey. As women we face different challenges when we are between endings and beginnings, in that place where difficult choices and shifting values are required of us. I wanted to shine the light of truth on the ingredients of the woman's journey of awakening that is often misunderstood and stigmatized by loved ones and society. My inner voice said, Begin it now! And so I did.

As a Ph.D. psychologist I'd been educated and trained in traditional Western scientific research methods. However, I wanted to hear directly from women, face-to-face, about their personal experiences of taking a journey to awakening by "leaving home," either physically or metaphorically. I wanted to illuminate the courage, strength, and wisdom that take a woman through the shedding of old roles, into the fallow emptiness, and toward birthing her true self. I did not specifically select participants for this study. Most of the participants found me, or I found them through a variety of serendipitous ways.

That same year I attended two gatherings of midlife women from across the country. I held a focus group at each gathering where I invited women to share their "leaving home" stories. Then I formulated a set of open-ended questions from which I conducted preliminary interviews, while continuing to refine my questions based on emerging themes. I spent one year conducting interviews with ordinary women who told me stories that were as extraordinary as they were universal. I ultimately audio taped and then transcribed verbatim the stories of sixteen women from different parts of the country. The tapes were then returned to each woman. The transcribing of taped interviews was tedious and time-consuming, but essential in order to identify key themes that emerged, and to select stories that best exemplified those themes. While each interview was unique, all were similar in three ways. Every participant said she had never before told her story, and the opportunity to share her story with an attentive listener was healing. I was particularly struck by the fact that each woman, when asked what was calling her, reported some version of a death theme—death of her soul, spirit or self. I was awed by the stories and grateful for the level of candor and trust. We were, after all, strangers to each other. To be a part of these interviews was indeed a privilege.

We each have many endings and beginnings in a lifetime. Some endings are forced by circumstances, some consciously chosen. You may have completed your transition by now, or are hearing the first heart whisperings, or you may be suspended between endings and beginnings. Whatever the nature of your journey—chosen or circumstantial—each path offers gifts when you are able to soften your resistance to entering the unknown. I invite you to become a sister journeyer and try answering the interview questions for yourself before reading the book.

## GUIDING QUESTIONS

1. What was calling you to "leave home?"
2. How did you prepare yourself to begin your transition?
3. Did any of these typical aspects of endings precede your journey?

*Disengagement*—a break in the familiar order of things (choice or circumstances),

*Disidentification*—the loss of identity or role(s); the inner aspect of disengagement,

*Disenchantment*—the discovery that a significant part of your reality no longer existed,

*Disorientation*—feeling lost, confused, no sense of a future; nothingness, sense of time or space has changed.

4. What have you had to deal with around loss and letting go?
5. Is forgiveness of self or other an issue? If yes, how have you handled it?
6. What have you learned about choices?
7. What was/is the most difficult part of your transition?
8. What sustained you during your transition between endings and a new beginning?
9. What is your current definition of authentic self? Of inauthentic self?

10. Has your image of home changed? If yes, what new symbols or images are you now aware of?

11. What tools (practical resources) have you found useful in making the transition?

12. What have been the gifts of your journey?

13. What is important for other women to know about embarking on a similar journey at midlife?

# *Introduction*

It happens to most women at midlife—the siren
call to deeper purpose and meaning, to something
more. You may hear it first as a whisper, or feel it as a
nudge, or a big bang. You might turn away in deep
fear of change or in simple avoidance. Or you can
perk up your inner ear in curiosity and listen deeply,
then courageously follow a primal thread into the
forgotten aspects of your self. If you follow this
thread it will lead you back to the beginning, toward
reclaiming the self you gave away in exchange for
love and acceptance, or lost without noticing, or cast
off like an old dress. Midlife is the time for reclaiming and rebinding the lost parts of your self into the
wholeness and feminine wisdom that the planet desperately needs right now.

Historically, a woman's midlife transition has not
been valued for its complexity, nor for the courage

and challenging choices it requires. This book sheds a compassionate light on the experiences of sixteen women who embarked on a midlife awakening by leaving home. This is not a book about divorce, although divorce can be part of the midlife equation. These women are not running away from something but toward something. That something, for each of them, is her authentic self.

*Endings. Beginnings . . . When Midlife Women Leave Home in Search of Authenticity* looks deeply at the midlife transition experiences of women who so desperately wished to know themselves that they were willing to risk everything, and in the process gained more than can be imagined. These are the voices of women finally free to tell the truth of their own lives. Their strength and humanity is marvelous . . . they are explorers in the true sense. Most had never before told their stories, but they learned that by telling our stories we can release the limitations of our past, empower ourselves, and transform outdated notions of aging, spirituality, creativity, feminine strengths, and diversity. This book blends true stories with feminist research, expert commentary, and my own personal quest to find true home within. I tell my own story in a series of snapshots of different periods of my life, organized around (what I now know to be) a spiritual quest that started with the sudden death of my child.

I have left home a few times and in the process have reinvented myself both personally and professionally. I have felt the slings and arrows of stigma, loss, and difficult choices and consequences. However, the journey has gifted me in many ways. With each home leaving I was broken open to spiritual truths and healing. It has made me a more compassionate woman, therapist, mother, friend, and grandmother. I have learned to be present with emptiness and the unknowns of life transitions, and I have also learned that *alone* is not the same as *lonely*. I always land on my feet because the universe supports my soul's evolution. I may not have the material status of some people, but I have earned a deep spiritual connection to myself.

I had spent years seeking wholeness through the study and practice of spirituality, and read a multitude of books on midlife transition both as a psychologist working with the human change process and as a woman trying to find my way. Yet I did not find the personal tools I needed to respond each time life called me to deeper meaning and purpose. The literature was fragmented. It was either not grounded in real women's experience or it simplistically focused on aspects of what truly is a complex journey. I was unable to find a map for the road ahead, either for myself or for the women I counseled. This book offers both practical and spiritual tools and insights for a journey that has historically been traveled largely in darkness.

Leaving home is a symbolic act of self-creation that opens the door to a woman's spiritual growth. The home leavings in this book were motivated solely by a failure to thrive and a need for something more. Each woman related a version of, "I felt like I was dying," "My spirit had died," or "I took a wrong turn somewhere and no longer recognized myself." Each woman responded in her own way to the shedding of old roles and ways of being that no longer served her evolving midlife self. A home leaving can be metaphorical in that a woman responds by staying within an established set of constraints while navigating the murky waters of deep inner change. Some leavings take the form of emotional withdrawal, the consequences of which are quite detrimental to the woman and her loved ones. Often the response is to physically leave whatever has been home to her— whether that's been ten years in a convent, fifteen years in the corporate world, or a thirty-year marriage—and embark on a journey to a life that meets her own evolving midlife needs.

For the first time in history, enormous numbers of women are crossing the threshold into midlife and looking toward an additional thirty or more years of life. These women now account for almost 30 percent of the American population, a number that continues to grow as the baby boomers age. Yet, the most neglected and misunderstood stage of adult development may be that of women aged fifty and beyond. These women grew up amidst major social change and contradiction: sex, drugs and rock 'n roll; disillusionment and rebellion; openness to change; and an unprecedented interest in self-development. More women over fifty are now starting businesses than those under fifty. Fifteen percent of women over sixty are choosing not to retire and are re-entering the work force with second careers. These are the same women who were protesting the Vietnam War. This is the "I can do anything I want" generation. However, this healthy attitude frequently generates a major detour at midlife—sometimes over and over. In my work as a psychologist I have heard women in midlife express the fear of becoming a "bag lady." Being a bag lady means being adrift with no money or other resources, or becoming homeless. When queried, these women often expressed feeling dependent on or loyal to a relationship or situation that no longer suited their deeper needs, combined with fear of making the necessary life changes. This underlying fear frequently represented a tension between the security of home and beloved relationships, and the call of the true self.

Women have very different needs at midlife than men. While we represent the largest segment of the contemporary adult female population, little is known about the unique challenges we face at midlife. I know both personally and as a practicing psychologist that midlife, for women, is a time of spiritual development. Life calls us to reclaim the true self we abandoned long ago in favor of acceptance, love, biological destiny, and security. But we do it in a way that is different from that which is recognized or understood. *Endings. Beginnings . . . When Midlife Women Leave Home in Search of Authenticity* is intended to inform, inspire and initiate the millions of baby boomer women entering midlife by scouting the territory ahead and revealing through first-hand accounts the real story. It endeavors to remove the mystery and misunderstanding that surrounds the female midlife transition and the process of personal change. My deep desire is to lessen the stigma that tragically limits or makes more difficult our personal and spiritual growth across the life span, and to re-frame the midlife transition as a normal stage of female development.

## THE STORIES

These stories have not been told before, and without stories there is no way to understand either the challenges or the gifts of the quest for authentic self, or the inner and outer elements that sustain such a quest. These are ordinary women who decided to step boldly into the fullness of their true selves and tell the truth about their journeys—the painful and the joyful parts. Each of the stories is really your story, told by another woman so that you may know yourself better and know you are not alone or different. The stories are framed around key emotional and spiritual themes that emerged in their telling. Each illuminates one of the many possible paths to authenticity and wholeness, while shedding new light on mechanisms involved in women's spiritual growth.

❖ Two artists struggled for years with blocked creativity until they faced the ways their conditioned roles sabotaged their artistic souls. For each woman, leaving home finally released her creative gifts and she was rewarded with the authentic artistic expression for which she yearned.

❖ Two women received wake-up calls in the form of health crises that propelled them toward quests of mythical proportions, and the poignancy of difficult choices and consequences they faced.

❖ Two women left the convent after many years, each in her own way, when the call to embrace their true nature became louder than the call to religious life.

❖ Two women relinquished custody of their adolescent children and ultimately were gifted with stronger, more loving and authentic relationships with them as adults. In the process each woman created a fulfilling career based solely upon the gifts of her leaving-home journey.

❖ Two women with tenacious commitments to finding and successfully bringing their authentic selves into the established constraints of their traditional roles and family relationships, eventually found gifts in that commitment.

❖ A woman experienced the death of her teenage son as it precipitated a life crisis that opened the door to her journey; and another began her journey with the loss of her cherished identity when her last child left home. The two women describe a similar journey through the deepest despair and depression, to spiritual awakenings and wholeness.

❖ A professional woman left home by withdrawing emotionally from an abusive partner and experiencing profound alienation from self and others, finally to face professional burnout and a near health crisis. You will learn how victimization, alienation, personal power, the false self, and love are all intertwined.

❖ A woman was orphaned as a child and completed her life-long search for true home when she finally integrated abandoned aspects of her self.

There is a story in this book that can strengthen and guide you, wherever you are on your journey. This journey to authentic self does not imply a destination. The notion of *self* is not debated or resolved in this book. Nor has it been resolved by the great "self versus no-self" spiritual debates of our time. This is a practical book that draws on psychological and perennial wisdom to support and validate any woman's journey to becoming the person she is meant to be. The book shines a compassionate light on the often misunderstood developmental process by which a midlife woman can achieve spiritual integration, glimpse wholeness, and taste authenticity. Share it with your girlfriends, your husband/partner, your therapist, your minister, your parents, and children. They will know you better and thank you for it.

The book is organized into four phases of the woman's journey.

## PREPARING TO JOURNEY

Phase I sets the stage for the core theme of the book—answering the midlife call to authenticity. By defining non-authenticity and showing all the ways that a false self is maintained, the book will help the reader more objectively open herself to the personal development work ahead. Chapter 1 examines three different paths the women in this study have taken to leaving home (leaving home being defined as any symbolic act of self-creation that opens the door to a woman's authentic self). Physical and metaphorical leavings, and emotional withdrawal, are understood through the stories of five women, including the author's personal story. Chapter 2 begins with powerful statements from women about why they needed to leave home: "I thought I was dying;" "My soul had died;" "I got my marching orders." The developmental concept of failure to thrive is explored. The chapter paves the way for introducing the process of birthing the authentic self. A Symptom Checklist serves as the compass and reference point for the journey ahead. It is a tool for raising awareness of the ways women maintain the false self, and serves as a way for the reader to rate herself in the privacy of her own heart. Chapter 3 identifies the nature of a calling and its relationship to authenticity, to midlife purpose and meaning. The women are introduced, and in their own words they describe the call that presaged their personal leaving-home journey. The conflicting social and psychological forces that inhibit women's authenticity are examined in light of cultural wounds that reinforce women's development and social conditioning. Seeing one's truth is framed as an act of courage that dynamically unfolds across the life span as a core aspect of authenticity.

## THE CALL COMPELS THE ANSWER

Phase II is about the essential emotional work of the leaving-home journey. Chapter 4 explores the tasks involved in taking the first step to leaving home, or crossing the threshold. For most women this is like going into the dark wilderness with no tools or map for the journey ahead. The archetypal descent process is then related to the modern midlife transition. Chapter 5 addresses the significance of the shadow's emergence at midlife. The Jungian concept of the human shadow provides a deeper understanding of the obstacles a woman can encounter when she begins to awaken. Specific ways the shadow maintains the inauthentic self are explored. Stories of compassion, choice and compromise illustrate the strength and determination of the women telling them. Chapter 6 shows how emotional work is part of a woman's midlife transition. Her spiritual growth requires that she work through loss, letting go, grief, guilt, and forgiveness. These elements are central to personal development and, as such, they are part of the journey to self. Women's ways of navigating these passages are woven throughout the chapter. Two powerful stories of forgiveness are explored, both of which were pivotal factors in the women's ability to finally cross the threshold.

## TOOLS FOR THE JOURNEY

In order for the journey to be sustainable—that is, for a woman to go all the way through it and resurface with the gift of her authentic self—a specific line of travel is asked of her. The three chapters of this section offer a map and tools for navigating the inner journey while at the same time being present for everyday activities such as work, relationships, parenting or playing. Chapter 7 is an inquiry into the history and politics of women's spirituality that places the journey in a contemporary context. Modern incarnations of ancient feminine spirituality are explored in terms of their relationship with nature, the environment, and the earth. Women's spirituality is recognized as the "fourth wave" of feminism—a fusion of spirituality and social justice; a spiritually informed paradigm of power based on a reverence for nature and the environment, mutuality, and political action that is guided and sustained by feminine values. In chapter 8, the perennial concepts of stillness and openness are demystified. Stopping, looking and listening are timeless spiritual practices that can sustain a descent into the groundlessness and the unknown of any transition. Specific practices embodying stillness and openness are explored in depth. Chapter 9 provides practical tools for supporting yourself through the everyday rigors of the journey. These are the everyday matters of re-creation, choice, attitude, money, health, and connection.

## THE GIFTS

Often a major life transition will be short-circuited because of the difficulties and obstacles encountered along the way, and the gifts may be forfeited. Because we cannot see clearly in the dark of transition we might run away, pull back, or force change before the fruit is ripe. When navigated with awareness and trust in oneself and in the basic goodness of life, a midlife transition offers many gifts.

Chapter 10 sheds light on the realities of a journey to authenticity. In this chapter the linear look of authenticity is redrawn to depict the circular, multi-layered, organic process of spiritual development that it really is. Chapter 11 delves into the elements of spiritual freedom. These elements include integration, wholeness, equanimity, and spiritual maturity. This is not to imply there is a final goal or destination—just the freedom to BE. Chapter 12 suggests that ultimately the journey to authenticity is about awakening to our essential nature and reclaiming those spiritual qualities that are our birthright.

*It doesn't happen all at once. It takes a long time.*
*That's why it doesn't often happen to people*
*who break easily,*
*or have sharp edges, or who have to be carefully kept.*
*Generally, by the time you are Real,*
*most of your hair has been loved off,*
*and your eyes drop out*
*and you get loose in the joints,*
*and very shabby.*
*But these things don't matter at all because*
*once you are Real you can't be ugly;*
*except to people who*
*don't understand.*

—Margery Williams *The Velveteen Rabbit*

*Preparing to Journey*

# ONE

# Ways of Leaving Home

*How do you know that you have moved,*
*or been moved?*

—Kati Pressman

Leaving home," for our purposes, refers to any symbolic act of self-creation that opens the door to a midlife woman's authentic self and to a spiritual journey toward more conscious living. The implications of leaving home are profound when a woman is leaving solely to free herself from ways of being for which she has been rewarded and accepted, but that no longer serve her evolving midlife self. She must leave behind the roles that had previously made her feel secure and loved. Ironically, when a woman leaves home in order to find true home within, she begins a descent into the very depths of her being that can take different outer forms.

The call to authenticity presents itself in many guises, and challenges women on many levels. Elsie said, "I didn't know what it meant that my various personae began crumbling at about age fifty." Now she knows she was being asked to see new truths about herself, her life, and her world. She was being nudged, and not too gently, toward the next level of growth.

Change is part of life. We must seek to welcome it for its potential for self-discovery and spiritual growth. Whenever and however a woman gets the message that the old roles and ways of being no longer fit, she is being called to awaken. If she misses the opportunity to respond she may spend the rest of her life hiding from herself. The woman who responds embarks on a solo voyage into uncharted territory and begins an adventure requiring courage, commitment and trust in the unfolding process. Either path, responding or not responding to the call to authenticity, brings its own risks.

When a woman has fulfilled a traditional female role for many years and later responds to the call, two things can happen. Her loved ones may balk and covertly refuse to relinquish their own privileged roles, needing her to remain in roles that no longer serve *her*. One woman quipped, "They wanted an electric mother, one they could plug in to perform, then turn her off until they needed her again." When stifling role expectations won't yield to the woman's need to grow and change, physically leaving may be the only choice.

Another option is that the woman's loved ones are willing to venture into the unknown with her and learn to trust the shifting shape of self and relationships she is initiating. The woman then leaves home metaphorically by going deeply inward to retrieve the neglected or abandoned aspects of herself. Her challenge then is to integrate the retrieved parts of herself into the milieu of her current life.

Both the physical and metaphorical home leavings involve a journey into the unknown. Each asks the woman to become a student of herself and her environment, to explore both inner and outer terrain. Both paths, of course, have many variations, depending on a host of factors that will come to light as these courageous women's stories unfold. While every story is different, each woman responded to the question, "What was calling you?" with some variation of the death theme. Several expressed the conviction that they were saving their lives by leaving home. One woman referred to being a bird let out of a cage. But whether she leaves home physically or metaphorically, each woman brings new life to herself and to her world. Clearly, whatever she risked for the sake of authenticity paled in comparison to the urgency of the midlife call to authenticity.

## PHYSICAL LEAVINGS

The majority of women interviewed were entrenched in relationships and roles that either couldn't or wouldn't yield to their yearning for growth. Faced with this dilemma, these women chose to physically leave home, familiar roles, and the security of cherished relationships. They broke the rules at a time of life traditionally characterized as one of integrating and settling into the golden years along with a vibrant silver-haired husband. Yet each set out on a solo journey of mythical proportions. Each woman consented to enter the unknown without a map of the territory ahead.

JACQUIE ✑ What drives a woman to leave that which she has spent her entire adult life building? I asked this question of Jacquie, a vibrant and wholesome woman who left a thirty-two year marriage to a man she dearly loved. "I was dying inside," she told me. After her three children were grown Jacquie worked for more respect and understanding from her husband, and for deeper communication. When none of these happened she became depressed. She removed her wedding ring, but knew that divorce was not the answer. She also knew that, "To remain where I was emotionally and spiritually, I truly would die." In desperation Jacquie prayed for a teacher. "I wanted to be led and empowered because I didn't know anything but the codependent-authoritarian model of adult relationships. I didn't believe there was a Jacquie I knew or liked very much, only the Jacquie my husband and children knew."

Jacquie's teacher appeared in the form of a women's spiritual group. After a few years of deep inner exploration, Jacquie realized that she was becoming a real person. Her authentic self was emerging. As she grew spiritually Jacquie longed for a space of her own where she could live and breathe. In her fifty-ninth year she announced to her family that she would take a sabbatical year for herself, a year without taking care of others. On the rainiest day of the year—the day the family dog died—Jacquie moved out of the family home into her own apartment. She took only minimal furnishings because she wanted to live her new-found values rooted in voluntary simplicity. In addition, she wanted to keep the family home intact for future traditional family gatherings.

Jacquie is one of several women I interviewed who left home physically but did not end her marriage relationship. She knew only that the relationship needed to be different, and she had to be stronger before she could return home. She worked hard at defining boundaries to meet her needs in the relationship, continued her spiritual growth work, and successfully supported herself. Jacquie sincerely believed it was possible to create a new relationship out of the old, but she needed to be physically separate in order to nurture and sustain her new beginnings. In her eyes, that was the only way to breathe new life into her spirit and her marriage.

My research uncovered a common thread among women who physically leave home: the sincere intention to cause no harm to their loved ones. As a result, the task of home leaving is filled with complexity and challenging choices. Most of these women had never lived alone before. The journey required each one to tap into her own deep well of strength. Ironically, through honoring the slow and sometimes painful process of spiritual growth, these women were gifted with a heightened sense of morality, ethics, and responsibility to and for actions taken. For Jacquie the challenge was to honor her own needs while giving her relationship the opportunity to grow with her, and to do this with integrity and compassion.

ANN ∞ After a thirty-year marriage and raising four wonderful children, Ann left home at the age of fifty-three. They were a close Catholic family and did everything together. It looked crazy to leave, she explained, because her former husband is a good person with fine qualities. She left because she needed to explore, to experiment in the world, to have room to express her true self. Why couldn't she do this within the context of the marriage? Because she had spent thirty years carrying the emotional responsibilities of the marriage, for making relationships work. Then she finally realized how low her self-esteem was and how much she had betrayed herself. "There was something about being with him that weakened me. I don't know how to explain it. He didn't do anything wrong, yet I felt as though I'd just had poison put into my system. How could I feel like I was suffocating and dying— when this man is such a good person? I see now that energetically I did the emotional work for him, and he did the calm, cool, collected thing for me. I didn't realize the depth of my role in holding up the family and the relationship until after I left."

Both Ann and Jacquie had followed the rules of the era in which they became women, and found that the traditional woman's role is a double-edged sword. They played by all the rules and do not regret their early choices, but they do recognize the hefty price they paid. Their spirits were caged. At midlife, having fulfilled the obligations they accepted as young women, each heard the call to spirit, purpose, and a deeper fulfillment than the traditional female role would allow. Once they answered yes to the call, there was no turning back.

Their stories illustrate the courage and strength each woman found within herself. As Ann explained, "The leaving process has been long and slow, filled with honest grieving. I didn't run away or fill myself up with busyness. There was deep loneliness, then pure terror. I didn't know what I was walking toward, just that it was the lesser of two pains. I could never have gone through this without the unseen forces I called upon to help me. I had no family support. What I did was very threatening to my mother, my married siblings, and my long-time women friends. It looked crazy to everyone but me."

Ann is an artist who longed to bring her art into the world. For thirty years she had based her identity on her husband and four children. She is now living alone for the first time in her life and loving it. As an artist she is rediscovering her innate self-worth, rather than depending on her family or her art to prove her value to the world. She knows that she must experience lots of different people and things in order to know her true self. "At first I felt like a bird in a cage who flies out, then returns to the perch, then stays out longer each time. Now there is no cage. I am doing things to see who I am, how I fit into the landscape. I am truly exploring all the edges through creative expression of myself, through singing, dancing, writing."

Both Ann and Jacquie believe they were saving their lives by leaving home. They exemplify the many women who make the choice to physically separate from the familiar roles, ideals and patterns that no longer meet their midlife needs. Women who make this choice, like Ann and Jacquie, are often misunderstood or stigmatized by loved ones and society. Not knowing what lies ahead, each has to plot her own course without a guide for the journey. They have only their strength, integrity and inner voice to guide them. They are explorers in the truest sense.

## METAPHORICAL LEAVINGS

The majority of the women I interviewed found it necessary to physically leave all that they loved in order to respond to the call of the authentic self. Yet not all women take this path. Some do not need to go anywhere. The journey to self can be accomplished within the context of their current lives and relationships. They can stay right where they are and go deep within themselves. They leave home metaphorically. This may appear to be the easier path, but it is not. The success of any metaphorical home leaving depends on both the woman's courage, and the understanding of her loved ones and their willingness to change.

KAREN ∞ Karen was fifty-nine when she began her metaphorical home-leaving journey. Her husband had recently retired as a well-known public figure in the community of her birth. Married for thirty-nine years, Karen had devoted her adult life to caring for a seriously mentally ill child, raising three daughters, and being the silent partner behind her husband's career success. For many years she thrived on the emotional dramas of both her mentally ill child and her husband's career. As each of those roles came to an end Karen got her first glimpse of how much she'd lived her life through others. "I'd adapted over time. I know the ways in which I compromised, but don't fully understand at what point I sold out. I still don't know when I crossed over," she said.

In the beginning Karen believed that actually leaving home was the only way to get enough freedom to redefine herself. For twenty years she had nurtured vague plans to leave home when she was no longer needed. As soon as that goal was in sight, Karen's elderly mother became ill and needed her care. So she left home metaphorically. She removed her wedding ring and decided to work toward change within the constraints of the marriage. For many practical reasons she valued her marriage, but the relationship with her husband no longer filled her need for a more authentic life. Removing her wedding ring was a symbolic act of recreating herself. I interviewed Karen one year into her metaphorical home-leaving journey. The wedding ring continued to be absent from her finger. She was finding ways to retrieve and explore undeveloped aspects of herself. She called it filling the holes. "I wanted them to hear me speak with a different voice, hear me out of my strength and not out of a plaintive wail. They had me figured out to be a certain person, and I was more than that. I needed to live from my core," she explained.

Karen explored metaphysics, creative writing, women's circles, traditional Native American ritual, ceremony, song and dance. As she watched how younger women in her support group resolved difficult problems, she opened to receive support from the spiritual world. She shifted away from Western medicine to alternative healing methods that enhanced her energy and health, and that addressed the underlying emotional issues of her transition. Karen took a major step toward authenticity when she refused to collude any longer with the multi-generational family denial of alcoholism and abuse. At this point she had begun to live her truth. She affirmed, "I've found a fullness that I gave up when I married a man who didn't understand these needs. Something has shifted in how I speak and how I see myself. I now feel free to trust my instincts."

Six months after our initial interview, I received a phone call from Karen saying she wanted to update it. When we met for lunch she proudly announced that she had put her wedding ring back on her finger during a women's circle. Thoughtfully, she explained her decision. "I was willing to risk everything by getting a divorce after thirty-nine years of marriage, in my hometown, where my husband is a public figure, while my family is expanding through marriages and grandchildren, when I had so much to lose—in order to salvage myself, to become authentic. When I was willing to do that and live with the unknown consequences—including family rebukes that I had messed things up—then the process had a life of its own. When the train comes to a screeching halt, even a bystander can feel the reverberations. My husband has not only honored all the things I said I needed in the relationship, showing that our relationship is valuable to him, but he has learned how to demonstrate its value to me."

Karen has rediscovered a passion for writing, a talent she put aside when she married. "Writing is my tool for speaking my truth. Now that I live from my authentic self I have something to write about." Karen realizes that her ongoing challenge is to protect her new-found authentic self so she doesn't retreat to the false self she left behind.

NANCY ∽ Nancy was forty-eight years old when she came into my psychotherapy office saying that she needed guidance or she would have to leave home. She and her husband married young, raised four daughters, and built a successful family-run organic farm. She has always been an equal participant in all aspects of the business and in creating their sustainable lifestyle.

She was catapulted into a crisis of authenticity while watching a television talk show on abuse. "I began to cry. Next morning I felt like I'd been beaten up. Didn't know what to do with that. As a child of alcoholics I have always tried to create the perfect reality I never had as a child. There was a lot of pain when I realized I had to change something inside of me that I'd never seen before—the way I dealt with relationships through rose-colored glasses, the way I overlooked things. Very painful. A veil was removed, a hole was socked in my reality, and I didn't have anything to replace it with. My choice was to find guidance or leave home—walk away from it all."

I interviewed Nancy nine years later in order to get her retrospective view of the ingredients of the journey that began when she came into my therapy office. Only five feet tall, she is one of the most courageous women I know. Once Nancy saw the reality of the inauthentic life she'd been living, once the veil was lifted and the false self revealed, there was no turning back for her. "I couldn't continue in the old way. I would have gotten sick and died. My soul was calling me to continue moving forward. I was hoping that the family I loved so much could make room for this to happen, and they did. But I had to initiate it. I had to take a chance. I couldn't do anything less," she explained.

What did she do? The most difficult part of the
transition was letting go of the fear of shaking things
up, of kicking a big hole in the superficial harmony
of her life. It was a long process of developing awareness of the habitual ways she maintained her inauthentic self, such as saying yes when she really meant
no, allowing her own needs to slide, accommodating
others to the point of being perpetually angry, blaming and resentful. Her husband was willing to change
his role and make more room for her to be herself.
Nancy's twenty-five-year practice of yoga and meditation gave her the necessary discipline to focus
inward, to go deep within herself and find her true
center. She said, "I had to take responsibility for
myself on all levels and let go of blaming others.
When we fall asleep or get too comfortable, we get
afraid. This journey requires constant awareness, to
not give in to the fear of losing our comfort zone,
fear of being vulnerable. Becoming authentic takes a
long time and is scary. Like ripping off your skin,
layer by layer, and exposing your heart."

Today Nancy is committed to taking responsibility for her truth at all levels. She and her husband
have two chairs by the window in their bedroom.
These are the truth-telling chairs. It's where they go
to council together. "It took some training to get him
to listen to me, to reinforce continually that, 'This is
not about you, it's about me. It's my turn.' He finally

got it, and now we share equal time. When I say I've
got a sore knee, he doesn't point to his sore elbow.
He asks about my knee. It was a process. Men have
to undo what we women trained them to do by not
being our authentic selves."

## WITHDRAWAL INTO NEUTRAL

A variation of the metaphorical home leaving is
what I call withdrawing into neutral. This period of
emotional disengagement can be a way for a woman
to retreat until she is ready for the inner work of
transition. Withdrawal into neutral allows a woman
to emotionally "leave" without having to face the
choices and consequences of leaving home. It also
signals a profound stuckness because it is a state of
paralysis of mind, body and spirit.

Withdrawal into neutral is the most painful and
self-destructive way to leave home. It jeopardizes
one's emotional, physical and spiritual well being.
This is what I did for several years before I had the
courage to risk moving forward when my emotional,
physical and spiritual well being depended on it.
And this is what my mother did. Perhaps this is what
you are doing.

In his classic book on life transitions,
William Bridges emphasizes the importance of the
neutral zone to any transition process. This fallow
period of emptiness is a normal but confusing

time of in-betweenness. It is a rich and scary place between disintegration and regeneration, between endings and new beginnings. This apparent dark hole of emptiness offers no familiar ground to stand on. What is asked of us is to give in to the fallow emptiness and not try to escape it, because it is richly essential to all life transitions. There is much work to be done here. It requires stopping, looking and listening. While feeling chaotic and frightening, this is where new beginnings take root. An openness to and trust in the unknown is required for a successful completion of the transition.

The withdrawal into neutral that I speak of as a way to leave home is characterized by an emotional shutting down, rather than opening to what is. It is a way to avoid facing the unknown. When a woman withdraws into neutral, it means she has applied the brakes somewhere in the process of disintegration of inauthenticity. She is stuck because she is unable to move forward, and yet cannot go backward. So she shifts into neutral. She puts her emotions in cold storage, closes her ears to the inner voice that is calling her, and shuts down because her inner conflicts are too distressing. She is actually emotionally paralyzed and stuck.

What keeps a woman stuck in neutral? Her emotional traps put her there and keep her there. These traps include her inner critic, unresolved fears, and all the ways she has compromised her authenticity.

Until she finds the courage to risk entering the unknown and trust her true nature, she is hiding. Each of the women I interviewed eventually reached a point where the pain of denying her real self was greater than the pain of leaving home. Emotional traps are explored in depth in chapter 5.

Nancy describes it beautifully. "Like a birth, I couldn't keep a lid on what was emerging, pushing out. This whole feeling of who I truly am was starting to come out, couldn't be stopped, and I didn't want to stop it."

MY STORY ∾ This book began as a personal inquiry into a long and difficult period in my life that, despite years of training as a psychologist, I did not understand. It was only after leaving all that had been home to me for fifteen years that I recognized I'd been stuck in neutral for half those years. Paradoxically, in an effort to avoid the dark places I simply created more darkness. And it is so difficult to see in the dark. We must trust our own evidence that our spirit is dying, and begin the journey before it gets too dark. I tell my story in hopes that it will help women recognize a destructive and difficult way of leaving home.

I am no stranger to the conflicts and anguish of a midlife home leaving. I, too, have felt the arrows of stigma pierce my heart and my resolve, the reproach of family members, and the utter terror of a free-fall into the unknown. Like many women, I have left home more than once in order to answer the call to continued growth and self-renewal. Each home leaving was preceded by a direct inner knowing that called me toward a lesson I needed to learn, an aspect of myself I needed to retrieve. Each home leaving has been a call to awakening.

Each call compels an answer. The hallmark of a true calling is that it will not leave us alone. We will not be free until we respond. After raising my son as a single mother I began to hear the whispers of my soul's longing for something more. This longing for wholeness and community persisted. After a series of confrontations with what seemed to be the meaninglessness of my life, I left home to live and work communally at the famed Esalen Institute in Big Sur, California. I was forty-four years old. It was a rich and rewarding three years of self-renewal for which I will always be grateful. At Esalen I healed from the earlier loss of my second child. I trained in massage therapy, luxuriated in the astounding power and beauty of the Big Sur coast, and was introduced to the world of humanistic psychology. I met and fell in love with the man I believed was my life partner, the person with whom I would spend the next phase of my life. I did not know that I was beginning a long journey that would eventually heal the part of me that was vulnerable to emotional abuse.

During those fifteen years with my partner, my life had the outer look of success and stability: a nice home on the California coast, a committed relationship, travel, community involvement, active social life. I had a clinical psychology practice and my partner had his own professional life. Over time I was subjected to increasingly extreme levels of emotional abuse by the man I loved and had committed to share life with. As the emotional abuse escalated I felt increasingly powerless to deal with his abusive anger. I was tormented by inner conflict, self-doubt and shame. The shame and anguish were compounded by the fact that I, as a professional psychologist, couldn't face what was happening in my own life. Like most abused women I didn't want to leave home, I only wanted the abusive anger to stop. And it didn't.

Somewhere along the way I withdrew into neutral. Neutral was my way of escaping the confusion and pain of a dark secret that was never witnessed by family or outsiders. Shutting down seemed to keep me safe from the self- hatred that engulfed and silenced me as I gave away my personal power, year after precious year of my life.

In the depths of my darkest despair I went to a monastery on the Pacific Coast to do a Winter Solstice solo retreat. My deepest yearning was to learn to "see in the dark" on that darkest night of the year. Throughout the night a wild coastal storm howled around my little retreat hut. I meditated and prayed to be able to pierce the veil of darkness that had swallowed me up when I withdrew into neutral. My little candle flickering in the dark seemed to be a beacon lighting my way, much like a coastal lighthouse guides storm-tossed ships home. I admitted powerlessness to find my way Home alone. All through that long, dark night I asked the Infinite Light within to show me the way, to light my path so I could see in the dark and find my way Home. Grace intervened and six months later I began the journey that has inspired this book.

Whenever we withdraw into neutral, we become alienated from our world and ourselves. Alienation and its indwelling darkness reinforce each other and create a vicious cycle. Because I was unable to see in my self-imposed darkness, I couldn't see how I was keeping myself stuck. I'd lost my ability to contact feelings, to self-reflect. No distinctions existed in that frozen wasteland. My bad feelings blended into a background of darkness and depression. I wasn't thriving. It was so dark within I couldn't see what I was doing to myself. I couldn't see my own emotional traps. This is the paradox of withdrawing into neutral as a way of leaving home. It is my personal definition of hell. And it could become yours if you choose to ignore the midlife call to awaken when it knocks at your door.

TWO

# Failure to Thrive

*What locks itself in sameness
has congealed.
Is it safer to be gray and numb?
What turns hard becomes rigid,
and is easily shattered.
Pour yourself out like a fountain.
Flow into the knowledge that what you are seeking
finishes often at the start, and
with ending, begins.*
—Ranier Maria Rilke, "In Praise of Mortality"

I felt like I was dying." "My spirit had died." "I needed to save my life." What kind of person makes
these statements? And why? I heard these expressions of truth many times from midlife women who

left home even though there was no obvious rationale for doing so. These women had the usual external trappings of a middle class life. Yet they felt they were dying because, on some essential level, they were not thriving.

"Failure to thrive" is a term typically attributed to babies and children. It originated with developmental psychology's study of children who failed to thrive physically and emotionally because of a profound lack of nurturing from their environment. Without normal attachment to other humans, these children did not grow or acquire language skills. Their development was stunted. This condition frequently led to death.

As I listened to one leaving-home story after another, I realized the women were describing a condition similar to that of undernourished babies. Each described an outwardly normal life that no longer nurtured her spirit and increasingly drained the life from her soul. In other words, she was not thriving to the extent that facing the terror of an unknown life was preferable to dying in her own home.

I am reminded of a dream I had several years ago. The dream came to me shortly after I betrayed myself by recommitting to a relationship that no longer nourished my spirit. In this dream I saw myself lying in a coffin while my blood slowly drained out of my body and dripped from a hole in the bottom of the coffin. Not only was I required to watch my lifeblood drain away, but I had also drilled the hole in the coffin. At the time I didn't understand my dream. I didn't want to see the truth: I had sentenced myself to a long, slow death of the soul. My unconscious was telling me in no uncertain terms that my soul was quietly hemorrhaging.

Most of the women I interviewed attributed their failure to thrive to being in roles or relationships that no longer served their emerging midlife needs. For others, failure to thrive resulted from careers that caged their spirits. Regardless of the cause, something profound was ending. That "something" was the activity or role around which their adult identities had been formed. Phyllis said, "All that had accumulated over my lifetime had to end in order for me to find myself, to rebirth myself." A woman's old identity needs to be shed when it no longer nourishes her emerging self.

A shift commonly occurs for women when their children go off on their own. Regardless of whether or not they have had a career, most women experience a crisis of identity at this time. Some never developed individual identities because they were preoccupied fulfilling their roles. This often isn't recognized until the children leave home.

Karen said, "I was so identified with living out the old script that I forgot to rescript." Jana had an awakening at age forty-five that led to leaving a twenty-five-year marriage to a fine man she loved, but who was unable to grow with her. "I had a career in the human resources field, but no clue as to the meaning of my existence once my mother role ended. I never developed an identity and didn't know my purpose or who I was." Jacquie describes it as a time of sadness and depression. "It's so hard being a mother. Unless you've been a mother, you can't imagine the loss of this role. A piece of me was missing and it left a vacuum in my life. If not mother, who am I?"

Each woman had spent her adult life willingly caring for others. When a woman defines herself through others, the feeling at midlife can be that of a starved spirit, which in turn can feel like death. In reality, it is the person she had become who wants to die. At the door to midlife she is called to stop and reclaim her authentic self.

Midlife ushers in a new developmental stage for women. This important stage is too often dismissed as a problem of menopause, the empty nest syndrome or depression. In our culture it is frequently considered a crisis to be medicated or fixed as quickly as possible. While a medical approach may be called for at times, a woman's midlife really is a time of spiritual opening and awakening. It is a time of ripening. It is a time for a new and different experience of "self." By the mid-forties a driving force begins to arise in women. This nameless force coincides with a normal decline in both reproductive powers and in the responsibilities embraced at an earlier time. Hormones no longer dominate and define. A primal creative energy that had been bound since puberty to reproductive cycles is now released, carrying with it an innate thrust toward authentic self-expression. This biological freedom releases a woman's yearning to express her deeper nature. For most women this yearning manifests as a crisis of meaning and purpose. Some find themselves bound to rigid roles and relationships that cannot meet their emerging need to embody the true self. This creates challenging choices. Some need to separate from loved ones. That which always felt secure and comforting now feels life denying, and they know it is time to listen to their hearts.

DIANA ∽ Diana, a mother of two sons, left home alone at age forty-five. "My soul was calling me for a very long time. Being Catholic made it hard to listen to my soul. I fought it, resisted it. But I was dying in a marriage in which our true selves couldn't come forth. Though living side by side, we each denied our true self. I'd been shut down, doing what was expected of me as wife, mother, and daughter—all those roles. Yet my creative self was emerging and I had to express it in the world. I had to save my life."

Whenever faced with a crisis of existence, we have three choices. We can choose physical death by suicide; or psychological death by shutting down emotionally; or we can choose the life that is calling to us. Torn between the security of the familiar and the yearning for something deeper, each woman I interviewed courageously chose on her own behalf. The potentially difficult consequences of this choice paled in comparison to the desperate need to know herself. Renowned theologian Mary Daly understood this when she said, "When the cow jumped over the moon, she didn't know where she was headed, just that she had to do it."

## ABOUT AUTHENTICITY

Authenticity is both a *way of being* and a *process*. For me, authenticity is when I gain congruence between my inner and outer, when I feel whole. Congruence means the public self mirrors the inner self, the outer reflects the inner, the flame and the shadow are one. You may have experienced a hunger for wholeness, for being more real. Rediscovering and reclaiming this wholeness is the *process* part of becoming authentic. It is the real work of the journey as attested to by the women's home-leaving stories.

Why is authenticity important? It is a positive attribute necessary for emotional and spiritual health. Paradoxically, authenticity is not encouraged by our society, particularly for women. This fact was illustrated by the classic study conducted two decades ago by the late Inge Broverman, a psychologist and professor in my doctoral program. Dr. Broverman asked people to describe characteristics of both a mentally healthy adult male and adult female. She found that the descriptions of a healthy male included the traits considered characteristics of positive mental health. But the characteristics of a mentally healthy woman included dependency, low self-esteem, a lack of assertiveness, and selflessness. These are actually the traits of self-abnegation and poor mental health.

Women continue to negate themselves in order to fit into the cultural norm. Self-abnegation actually prevents a woman from recognizing and reclaiming her real self. A former NASA aerospace engineer, Wendlyn Alter made a mid-career change and began writing on women's spiritual nature. In an article for The Qwest magazine, Alter says, "Self-abnegation in a woman is a traditional mechanism for strengthening her attachments to husband, children, household, community—all that keeps her locked securely in the grip of the ordinary, the small self, like a fly in a spider's web." That small self is the part of a woman that needs to please others to generate self-esteem. In a culture that already devalues the feminine, women are taught to rely on external authority and to look outside themselves for validation. The process of becoming authentic requires a woman to move beyond the small, people-pleasing self and to reclaim her inner authority. This is particularly challenging because women tend to define themselves through their relationships. Herein lies the deadly split. In a system that does not work for most women, that devalues the feminine, how can a woman be a whole person and retain beloved relationships? How can she navigate the chasm between her own needs and cultural norms?

The woman who embarks on this mysterious journey to reclaim her true nature is often stigmatized because she is rewriting the rules of the game. Not only is she frequently misunderstood by friends and loved ones, but she doesn't know where the journey is taking her. The path is traveled largely in darkness with little guidance and with significant stigma. She makes a leap of faith that is supported solely by life's longing for itself. Phyllis describes her own lonely struggle. "Facing this emptiness is difficult. I can't rely on my family during this time. I feel stigmatized and misunderstood. Even though we are very close, they are judgmental, do not understand what I am doing, and are frustrated with me. So I stay away and forego the emotional support I need so much right now." Phyllis left home at age fifty-three because she was called to follow her heart, her inner guidance. Yet she struggles with an inner critic that says she should conform to her family's need to keep her in the old roles and relationships that were draining her life force.

This journey is one of personal development. The inner work has many facets and will differ for each woman, but the basic task is learning to walk straight and true. Loosely defined, authenticity is being completely who you are.

Each woman I interviewed shared her current definition of authenticity. The responses included: "Being without mask or facade;" "The absence of self-deception;" "Being free enough of conditioning to be the self I would more naturally be;" "Living consciously from my inner wisdom, from my inner direction;" "To inhabit my own soul with peace and unabashed honesty." Phyllis discovered that, "Authenticity is the self that is revealed only after I rid myself of the soot that has filled all the crevices of my being. So much of my life experience was like a cloud covering the genuine me. I kept those experiences inside and they buried my true self."

Many women stressed the importance of not confusing honest self-expression with being hurtful. One woman emphasized that, "Authenticity does not mean rudeness, thoughtlessness, tactlessness, or insensitivity. It means knowing and being true to oneself, and living according to the teachings of one's deeper nature. It is developing oneself by stretching and growing in directions in which one feels pulled or propelled." Expressing yourself authentically means responding impeccably and with integrity to the events and people in your life. It is not a license to harm others, yet it means being truthful with yourself. Your responsibility is to use discernment and good judgment to decide how, when, where and to whom you express your truth. When women free themselves of obligations that deflect from their midlife unfolding, they can learn two things. First, we are each a random assortment of life events, relationships and dreams which have more or less assembled over the years. Second, our lives are actually ours to shape and make fit, as only we know how best to do. There are many curves and pitfalls on this road. The women whose stories are woven throughout this book are your guides.

## ABOUT INAUTHENTICITY

We must first recognize the many faces of inauthenticity in order to open to our real self. The inauthentic self is the face we have learned to present to the world, a persona. Sometimes it is called the personality or the false self. In the course of growing up, each of us adopts a persona in order to meet the expectations of parents, teachers, the workplace, religion and society. We learn at an early age that certain ways of being are acceptable while others are not. We adopt traits that are acceptable because most of us want the approval of others. The result is a false self.

In his book *Waking the World*, Allan Chinen says,

"Symbolically, it is often a woman's false self that society recognizes and honors, not her true self. Women are rewarded for being thin, beautiful, nurturing and accommodating—not for speaking their minds, insisting on what they want or heeding what their bodies need." Our culture rewards women for being inauthentic. Yet it is only the authentic self that is whole and complete; the false self is incomplete.

My dear friend Kathleen is both a published author and a psychotherapist. She spoke candidly about the false self as she understands it. "I may not always be aware when I am speaking or acting from my false self because I have been behaving this way from early childhood in order to earn acceptance and love. I believe I am *real* or *true* or *authentic* because this is the way I have behaved for as long as I can remember. However, I can often sense when another person is being false to themselves and me. I have a feeling of unease because what they are saying or doing does not match the feeling tone of their voice or their body language. Sometimes this incongruence is subtle and sometimes it is very obvious. This mismatch causes me to feel a range of unease from curious discomfort, to feeling seriously walled off and disconnected from the other person, to fearfully unsafe.

"From a spiritual perspective I do not judge this behavior as bad or wrong in myself or others as we are all being as authentic as we are able to be in each moment given our history and skills. From my center of unconditional love I feel compassion for the true self who feels unloved and is in hiding. I know the false self is only trying to protect me from feeling more rejection and loss of love. I know this because I have felt the pain of rejection when I have expressed my true feelings and needs and been criticized, judged, rejected or maybe even humiliated and shamed. When this happened too often in child-hood, my false self became stronger and more clever at hiding my true feelings and needs. As I learn to love myself more and become more self-reflective, I can sense this unease in myself and recognize that I am hiding my true self."

What Kathleen is saying is that when we are in the middle of the life story we are living out, we may not even be aware of its inner complexity. Like the fish that doesn't know its environment is wet, it is difficult to recognize the ways in which we have been conditioned. Finding out who you really are is not simple. There is so much you must feel your way through—and that takes time. The time it takes is the time you need. It is easier to move forward when you recognize where you are right now. A good place to begin is by looking at three ways through which you interact with the world. These are your *thoughts*, *behaviors*, and *feelings*.

## WAYS OF THINKING

DENIAL ⁓ Denial is the most common way of coping with difficult times. It is a way of thinking that distorts the truth, a failure to face and defend what you subconsciously know to be true. In denial you avoid certain issues or people and see things only as you want them to be, rather than accept them as they are. Remember my coffin dream? My unconscious was speaking the truth while I was in deep denial. In denial we abandon ourselves to keep the peace rather than speak our truth. We are unable to create healthy boundaries that protect, nurture and sustain the authentic self. This is the ultimate in self-betrayal. Women are particularly vulnerable to this pattern because of our conditioned role as nurturer and peacekeeper of relationships.

Most major spiritual traditions agree that denial separates us from our true nature. It is a form of self-delusion that creates disorientation and disempowers us. Underneath denial is the fear that we are incapable of handling conflict or accepting the truth. This fear makes ordinary problems even more powerful and persistent because we are fighting reality as though it were our enemy. Ultimately, the problem persists until a crisis of some sort forces us to deal with it. For some women it erupts in the form of an emotional crisis.

A well-educated professional woman, Linda was

astounded when her denial was unexpectedly lanced like a boil. She was attending a family education conference when, to her dismay, she found herself sobbing throughout a presentation on childhood abuse. After the lecture, she expressed bewilderment at her tears to the presenter. He asked if she had been abused as a child. Linda said, "I exploded inside and ran from the room. I screamed in my car all the way home." That lecture was the beginning of a long road and inner work that enabled Linda to break her forty years of denial of the sexual abuse in her childhood.

Once the cloud of denial surrounding her childhood abuse was lifted, Linda's life changed dramatically. Other aspects of her life that she denied came into sharp focus. The veils were lifted. Family patterns adopted long ago unraveled as she faced a lifetime of denying her truth. She saw that denial had kept her in destructive intimate relationships. "I would do anything to have a more authentic life. It has been like living in a glass bubble, scratching the glass with a tiny pin, until finally the hole was big enough for me to climb out." One of the gifts of climbing out of her glass bubble of denial was Linda's ability to confront and forgive her abusive father shortly before his death.

SHAME ∾ Shame is pervasive in our culture. It is the root of self-hatred because you think you are somehow not good enough. There is a deep sense of separateness similar to being in the glass bubble Linda describes above. In fact, shame has often been defined as feeling alienated and alone, as if behind a glass wall. Many women have been taught to feel shame about their bodies, their sexuality, their talents, their wants and needs, their intuition, their feminine values and their spirituality. Shame bedevils women who have been sexually abused in childhood or victims of domestic violence in adulthood. Perpetually denying your feelings and ignoring your truth eventually leads to despair and alienation. This despair is really a longing for connection to something deeper. It is the call to authenticity that asks you to let go of the illusions and denial in your life. Recovery from shame begins with daring to speak the truth as you know it, loving and accepting yourself just as you are, and listening to your heart. The exercise at the end of this chapter can help you begin the process.

## WAYS OF BEHAVING

SELF-BETRAYAL ∞ Self-betrayal completes the circle begun by shame. It disconnects you from aspects of yourself you have been taught are unacceptable. It undermines and blocks your creativity, your capacity for intimacy, and your awakening at midlife. It separates you from your true self. Living in ways that dishonor and devalue you is self-betrayal. Denying your truth is self-betrayal. Settling for something less is self-betrayal. Not expressing yourself authentically is self-betrayal. Avoiding responsibility for your feelings, thoughts and actions is self-betrayal. All the ways a woman betrays herself lead to resentment, self-hatred, grief and depression. When you betray yourself, so does the world. In her book *Something More*, Sarah Ban Breathnach compares women's behaviors of self-betrayal to a "spontaneous combustion of the soul."

For most women the root of self-betrayal is the learned need to be loved and accepted at any cost. Some women spend a lifetime trying to prove their worth by doing things to show the world they are okay. This is a cruel paradox because self-betrayal ultimately circles back in the form of self-hatred and shame. Shame and self-hatred are the seeds of self-betrayal. It becomes a vicious cycle. It is easier for a woman to hate herself than to feel the grief she carries for a lifetime of self-betrayal. The depression that visits many women at midlife is frequently repressed grief over having betrayed and lost herself. The only exit is the door marked "self-acceptance."

DOING-NESS ∾ A common theme in women's stories is the "doing-ness" of their lives, the busy-ness that has always given their lives meaning and purpose. The pace and sheer quantity of responsibilities in many women's lives is formidable. Demands of family, career, community and personal relationships compete with quality time for the self. Most of us in this hurry-up, instant response culture are feeling the same sense of overload, yet we dare not slow down for fear that the whole show will collapse. Or we wonder, *who would I be if not a doer?*

Midlife can bring to a screeching halt the familiar pattern of doing too much, too fast, for too many. When this happens, a woman is apt to blame herself for feeling unable to cope with the fast track of her life. This is because it looks and feels like the same old problem of simply being too busy, and in the past we have been able to handle it all with our usual coping strategies. But the reality is that we can't—and believing we can is really the problem.

Elsie describes herself as a big survival person who mostly worked two or three jobs as a nurse while raising her family. "From day one I learned that I must keep cracking or I wouldn't survive." A big piece of Elsie's transition has been to stop all the doing and to not push herself. She mused, "Maybe for women the home has to go because we are always so busy with inane stuff that we forget to ask the important questions—what do I want, what do I need?"

The doing-ness of women's lives is both externally and internally imposed. It keep us exhausted, resentful, guilty, and out of touch with ourselves. Chronic busyness steals our real self. Only you can decide to give yourself the gift of slowing the speeding train of your life. Chapter 8 offers many tools for how to stop when you have to keep going. Can you identify one thing you do that fuels the chronic busyness of your life?

## WAYS OF FEELING

Society expects certain things from girls but not boys, and vice versa. For instance, it is okay for girls to cry and feel hurt, but they should not get angry. It is okay for boys to be angry, but not to show vulnerability or hurt feelings. It is not acceptable for women to be selfish, but men can be selfish. This cultural cross-wiring encourages both women and men to be inauthentic. True feelings are rejected, repressed and relegated to our psychic underworld. They become part of our shadow side that is explored in chapter 5. Could this be why our prisons are filled with an overabundance of men and our mental health treatment programs with women?

Repressing and rejecting feelings is one reliable barometer of inauthenticity. When you disown your feelings you are disempowering yourself. Many respected and high-achieving women live inauthentic lives because they have disowned their feelings in order to maintain high-status roles or relationships in which there is no room for the real self. Connie is a nurse who has been in recovery from drug and alcohol addiction for ten years. She left home at age fifty-two and describes the process of reclaiming her feelings. "Intellectually I know my feelings are grown up feelings, but by the time they get from my head to my heart I feel confused, small and helpless. It's very scary to sit with my feelings, yet each time I do I realize I will survive. I'm still here. What's important is that I am doing it."

Two common side effects of disowned feelings are depression and psychosomatic illness. It is no wonder that these disorders have a much higher incidence among women than men. Not surprisingly, a component of depression and psychosomatic illness is the loss of personal power. Yet for a woman to relinquish personal power is entirely acceptable, while declaring her truth is far more stigmatizing.

DEPRESSION ∞ Depression resembles grief in that loss and sadness dominate the emotions. In addition, there are specific symptoms that affect sleep, thinking, appetite, energy level and behavior, often accompanied by a sense of hopelessness and worthlessness. There are two kinds of depression—exogenous and endogenous. Endogenous depression comes from within. It is related to the person's biochemical makeup and can be successfully treated with medication in most cases. It can be triggered by a severely disturbing event that impairs the brain's ability to function normally. This kind of depression is acute, may last for a long time, and usually responds to medication.

Exogenous depression is different. It is caused by external life situations and is the most common cause of depression today. It is a reaction to a significant loss that is perceived as harmful or devastating, such as loss of a relationship, job, reputation, or meaning in life. There is an accompanying anger that becomes turned inward, and soon anxiety joins the depression. This type of depression frequently emerges at midlife. It springs from a general discontent with one's life and a belief that what is left of life is not worthwhile. These thoughts are usually partially or completely out of awareness. Women whose entire identity has been tied to love and relationships, or to a marriage that has deteriorated, often experience at midlife a loss of meaning and purpose. All is slipping away and is about to be lost. Worry, anxiety, agitation and sleeplessness are common symptoms of this type of depression.

Dana Crowley Jack conducted a landmark study of the roots of women's depression. She investigated how internalized cultural expectations about being female affect women's behavior in relationships and how this can precipitate a plunge into depression. She interviewed women who described an either/or tension between sacrificing their own needs in order to preserve a relationship, and expressing their true feelings at the risk of losing valued relationships. These women censored their feelings, devalued their experience and repressed their anger. They silenced themselves. The depressed women in Jack's study did not communicate their real feelings. Outwardly they were falsely compliant, while inwardly they carried resentment, rage, anger and hostility. Any expressions of anger led to self-recrimination, shame and guilt. The women then redoubled their efforts to repress their feelings, falling into chronic depression.

Depression is intricately interwoven with repressed anger and grief. When there is no way to deal effectively with situations that frustrate, enrage or hurt you, or when expressing your feelings could be dangerous, then depression comes to help silence the rage impulse. It takes considerable psychic energy to withhold anger. The more feelings you hold in, the more depressed you can become. Silencing the feelings silences the true self. Constraining normal feelings such as anger and hurt hinders the expression of *all* feelings, both positive and negative. This deprives a woman of her passion and joy. Passion and joy are essential to authenticity.

For many women, depression is experienced for the first time at midlife. In this culture, midlife depression is often treated medically as a hormone deficiency. Many women do benefit in the short term from hormonal therapy, but a solution of greater magnitude is usually called for. The woman's midlife journey is really about change on all levels: physical, emotional, mental and spiritual. Midlife naturally calls you to awaken and develop greater depths of self-awareness. Whenever you turn away from this midlife call there are consequences. I learned this from my mother. I can almost pinpoint the day in her fiftieth year when my mother shut down and became depressed. I watched her live the next thirty years of her life a withdrawn, medicated victim of depression, headaches, and chronic pain. How might her life have been different if my beautiful, intelligent mother had trusted and valued her self enough to risk being more?

PSYCHOSOMATIC ILLNESS ∽ Psyche means spirit or soul. Soma has to do with the physical body. Psychosomatic illness is a term for physical pain that cannot be fully explained by a known medical condition. In psychosomatic illness, the repressed pain of the spirit expresses itself physically. It appears in a variety of forms: unexplained pain at several different sites in the body; gastrointestinal symptoms; sexual or reproductive disorders; and unexplained, vague neurological symptoms. As mentioned earlier, psychosomatic illness affects primarily women. A recent study by Nancy Henry presented to the 2009 American Psychosomatic Society annual meeting found that wives in tense marriages were more prone to risk factors for heart disease, stroke and diabetes than their husbands. The couples in Henry's study were married 27.5 years on average. The study suggests that relationship factors and emotional distress are related in women to high levels of blood pressure, blood sugar and triglycerides; to bulging waistlines; and to low levels of good cholesterol. Although husbands in unhappy marriages were also depressed, they did not show signs of physiological damage to their heath. In Henry's study, a link between chronic negativity, depression and metabolic disturbances was found only in the women.

The physical body often issues a wake-up call that encourages rebalancing. Rebalancing is a necessary step to recover from the conflicting and paradoxical roles that unbalance a woman and often bring her to the breaking point, both physically and emotionally.

ELSIE ∞ Elsie's story illustrates this beautifully. The eldest of eleven children, Elsie was raised on an Iowa farm. She learned early in life that she had to figure things out and do it all herself. She was a Catholic nun for nine years before marrying and having a family. A nurse by profession, Elsie always worked hard to support her family. At age fifty-six, divorced for fifteen years and her two daughters grown, Elsie experienced a three-year health crisis that forced her to rebalance.

"I'd been a consummate homemaker—loved cooking and caring for my home. The mantle of responsibility when I walked into my house never left me, day or night. I became profoundly weary, not sleeping much. Then I began feeling ill and pulled back. I could feel things crumbling." Elsie developed a series of physical ailments: mysterious allergies, symptoms of chronic fatigue, depression and anxiety. She tried every antidepressant with no success. She gave up participating in Western medicine because it no longer worked for her. She needed health care that listened and paid attention to her. Elsie began exploring how to live from her heart instead of her head. She had no idea what that meant, except that all the things that previously defined her had to go. She sold her beloved home of twenty-five years, gave away everything, and has not created another home because her quest is to learn to trust her inner guidance. The barrage of chronic ailments has been Elsie's teacher. Learning to ask herself over and over "What do I want?" has been her lesson. "It took something this severe to push me to look within. It's not a place I'd ever have volunteered to go. I had to become so debilitated that I believed I had no choice. Without this unnamable health crisis I wouldn't have entered my inner classroom." Elsie was being forced to rebalance herself by befriending her inner guidance. You, too, can begin to connect to your inner guidance.

Midlife brings many gifts and opportunities to help you grow emotionally and spiritually. Learning to stop, look and listen is one of them. You must be quiet to hear your inner voice. It begins with listening to your heart instead of your head. In your head you will find old admonitions about how you are "supposed" to be, worries and doubts and fears that are self-perpetuating. When you use your mind, you struggle and fight. It has been said that in prayer we speak in words and sentences, in meditation we listen. This is what meditation is—a listening. Some call it the inner voice that we listen to. In meditation, we feel this voice as the voice of our heart. All spiritual traditions consider the heart to be the great universal connection. By listening to your heart you will be guided toward your authentic feelings and needs, which in turn guide you toward nurturing and accepting yourself, and then toward uncovering your authentic self. To truly listen, you need to make yourself quiet. The following exercise will get you started.

## CONNECTING WITH YOUR HEART

Find a time and a quiet place that is yours and where you can be without interruption. Make the space as inviting and nurturing as you can, perhaps using pillows, music, and candles to invite relaxation. When you are comfortable close your eyes and put your mind in your breath. Watch the inflow and outflow of each breath. Listen to every sound, every external noise, noticing without analyzing or reacting. Just let them be there. Then feel your breath as an energy flow, moving in and out of your heart—a flow of love in and of gratitude out. Let your breathing heart effortlessly and gently refocus your attention each time your mind wanders into thinking. As you concentrate on your heart, ask your inner voice to guide you, to speak to you. Then watch your thoughts. Which is mind chatter and which is the voice of silence? If it truly is your heart speaking, then you will feel joy and connection to something larger than your small self. Continue to listen in this way for as long as is comfortable for you. Ten or fifteen minutes a day is sufficient.

## INAUTHENTICITY SYMPTOM CHECKLIST

This checklist can help you begin to identify the ways you are inauthentic. In the privacy of your own heart, check the "symptoms" of inauthenticity that apply to you. If you have other indicators of inauthenticity, you can add them to the checklist. You are the expert on YOU!

_____ Fear of rejection or abandonment

_____ Sense of despair or not wanting to live

_____ Yearning for something unnamable

_____ Loss of meaning, joy, or passion

_____ Difficulty tolerating your feelings

_____ Symptoms of depression

_____ *Please disease* (saying yes when you mean no)

\_\_\_\_\_ Unexplained physical ailments
\_\_\_\_\_ Difficulty knowing your truth
\_\_\_\_\_ Difficulty accepting yourself
\_\_\_\_\_ Difficulty setting boundaries with people
\_\_\_\_\_ Addictions (food, love, drugs, work, sex)
\_\_\_\_\_ Unexplained anxiety
\_\_\_\_\_ Self-abnegation
\_\_\_\_\_ Shame
\_\_\_\_\_ Self-hatred
\_\_\_\_\_ Guilt
\_\_\_\_\_ Chronic busyness
\_\_\_\_\_ Sense of alienation from yourself and others
\_\_\_\_\_ _____
\_\_\_\_\_ _____
\_\_\_\_\_ _____

# THREE

# Calls, Conflicts, Courage

*And the time came when the risk to remain tight in a bud*
*Was more painful than the risk it took to blossom.*

—Anais Nin

Callings are inner promptings that offer guidance for living more authentically, for waking up to true self. They beckon us toward the wisdom of our true nature. In the deepest sense, a true calling is an image of the wholeness already imprinted on your soul that keeps surfacing until answered. It is the inner compass of your life at work, the subtle voice of awareness. In either a shout or a whisper, it always asks you to pay attention to what is out of balance in your life that needs to be changed. It will guide you to heal the split in awareness that keeps you out of touch with true self. A calling can present itself in many disguises: perhaps a health crisis, or a vague feeling that something is missing in your life, or being burned out in a job or relationship. Living a "called life" means living an authentic life because you are paying attention to what is stirring in you. Hearing a call at midlife is a normal, natural event. It is not to be thwarted without consequences to the spirit. Yet sometimes when the call is answered a consequence can be a fall from grace with loved ones. However it expresses itself, a call compels an answer.

WAKE-UP CALLS

Frequently at midlife a woman experiences a wake-up call that expresses itself as a health problem, but is really a call to spiritual growth. She can develop disease when her personal growth process has been derailed or she doesn't pay attention. Unresolved personal conflicts can emerge as chronic, low-level irritability, stress and resentment that contribute to physical illness. It may be that she has repressed her feelings for too many years. Or that she has developed ways of thinking about herself and others that diminish and undermine her true nature. Or that she has been on a path of self-betrayal by not noticing that her life is out of balance and needs to change.

Elsie suffered from mysterious allergies, chronic fatigue, depression, and an anxiety she attributes to living in survival mode much of her life. Elsie said, "I was being called to learn to trust. It was so scary to let go of control. I'd wiped out my adrenals from a lifetime of worrying about what I should be paying attention to. Hyper-vigilance had wrecked my health. My body was saying stop." I asked Elsie how she answered her call to healing. "It's still very complex. I chose to sell my home and not get another place to live. I stayed with friends and used my money to rebalance my life. As a former nurse I hate what's happened to our health care system, and I couldn't take that route because it didn't work for me. I ultimately decided to forego insurance, mammograms, pap tests and such because I needed somebody to listen and pay attention to me. Currently I do things that help me be in the now. I watch the scared little girl within trying to come out and play. My process is to live in the present and learn to love myself. I can take care of others, but it is so difficult to love myself."

Clinical practitioners have known for years that the connection between feelings and physical health is direct and powerful. The mind-body connection has only recently been accepted in the Western medical model. Christiane Northrup, M.D. affirms that the way we perceive stressful events of our lives has more to do with our physical health than the events themselves. It has been well documented by medical research that certain patterns of emotional vulnerability affect specific systems of the body. For instance, studies on breast cancer show that feelings of powerlessness in significant relationships and an inability to express the full range of emotions increase some women's risk of developing breast cancer and can affect cancer survival rates. Many studies demonstrate a link between difficulties in handling negative emotions, especially hostility, and death from heart attacks. Further, the immune system can be compromised by lack of social support, loss of or separation from loved ones, or difficulties balancing a feeling of belonging with hard-won independence. Women who listen to our culture of driven-ness may take on the male psychology of power and achievement at any cost. This eventually brings suffering because it obscures the feminine principles of connection and creation. Mind-body research clearly shows a direct connection between physical illness, chronic pain, emotional disorders, and ignoring aspects of our lives that need to change.

While in the throes of my own decision to leave my home and partner of fifteen years, a friend recommended I consult a well-known and respected psychic, and I did so. Upon entering the psychic's consulting room she announced to me, "Your root chakra is turned backwards. What are you doing to yourself?" She proceeded to describe the emotionally abusive relationship that was draining my life force and proclaimed that I would develop breast cancer if I did not change my life immediately. That quickly scared me into action I'd been avoiding.

REBECCA ∞ When we met, Rebecca worked as a financial services consultant for a large corporation. She experienced a difficult childhood and had disconnected from her body for a very long time. Challenges in her nineteen-year marriage catalyzed a major life transition for Rebecca. During several losses of loved ones, her husband was unable to give her the closeness she needed. She developed migraine headaches, then uterine cancer. After surgery she began a course of biofeedback and meditation training. During this period she had a dream in which a bus ran over her and she awoke in a mid-eastern desert marketplace. She was walking through the market with other women when a male image emerged and said "I'm going to kill you." In the dream Rebecca crossed her arms and spoke loudly, "No you won't!" At the same time there was a dense, heavy vibration throughout her body and she heard the message, "If I am going to live I must be fully in my body." This was Rebecca's call to heal the split between her body, mind and spirit.

Rebecca now believes this was the beginning of her ability to reclaim her voice and her Self. She embraced the new energy vibration and found it to be a wonderful part of her. Over time the vibration has become lighter as transformation has progressed, though it can still be intense at times. After Rebecca's cancer surgery her relationship with her husband changed dramatically. She left home, but they maintained a commuter relationship. She found she liked the freedom and loved the intuition and spirituality that blossomed with the new connection to her body. Rebecca ultimately left the corporate world and her husband, became a certified Reiki bodywork practitioner. She answered the call to heal the alienation from her body and found her life's path working with the labyrinth—an intuitive, feminine spiritual tool—and sharing it with others. Chapter 7 discusses the resurgence of the ancient labyrinth as a contemporary spiritual tool.

It is true that at midlife the risk for physical illness increases. There are many reasons for this. On one level, it may be easier for a woman to get sick than to face the losses necessary to live a life that expresses her true self. Some rationalize that they should learn to be content, since their lives are halfway over. Some will trade their well being for financial security. The unknowns of change and transformation are far more frightening at fifty than they were at twenty. Take some time right now to examine what your own rationalizations might be.

JANA ∾ Jana was age forty-seven and had been married for twenty-five years. She'd known her husband since age fifteen, and she moved from her parental home into her marriage home. She said, "I had never developed an identity, didn't know my purpose or who I was, and had no clue as to the meaning of my existence once my mother role ended. I had a history of learning through my health problems: multiple surgeries, including eight on my knees and horrendous rehabilitation periods, chronic phantom pain, painkillers and anti-depressants. It got so bad I knew I needed to end the pattern." Jana experienced a wake up call, which she described as a sense of urgency to find her purpose and meaning. "One day while out walking in a field I fell face first, found myself bleeding profusely and nobody around to help. I prayed to God to either tell me why I am here or I am leaving. My life was ending—spiritually, mentally, physically, emotionally. I knew I was dying and must do something about it."

Jana entered a program of physical therapies, including very powerful breathwork training that led her to a sudden spiritual awakening. A year later Jana and her husband of twenty-five years parted amicably and continue to be close friends. "With my daughter leaving home I realized my husband and I had been living as best friends. For the last fifteen years we didn't have an intimate relationship and never discussed it. Outwardly, we appeared to be the perfect American family." Jana has not been to a medical doctor since leaving home and is now almost pain free. She has become more aware of her illness patterns as she has awakened to the spiritual dimension of life. She now realizes that her pain and illness had continued to escalate until she finally paid attention to their message. She believes she was near death before waking up to the call to heal her life on all levels. "It was definitely a blessing in disguise," she reflected. From this experience has come a new career for Jana as a breathwork facilitator, helping others deepen their contact with their inner selves.

Healing requires letting go of the familiar and stepping into the unknown. It may mean challenging belief systems and daring to break taboos. So much of what illness is about is the mind's clinging to the things it thinks it needs, and much of what we regard as success is the accumulation of things that support this way of thinking. Traditional medicine tends to reinforce conventional ways of thinking. You cannot change by continually stepping into a place that is already known. You really have to step into a previously unknown level of consciousness and way of being in the world. And this is scary. It involves reconnecting with lost aspects of yourself, listening to your inner voice, and moving out of the darkness of fear that holds us all captive. This has been true for each of the courageous women who shared their leaving home journey with me.

Rebecca, Elsie and Jana are women who experienced wake-up calls through health crises. Each woman was called to listen to her body and each had the courage to respond to the message she was being given. Each was required to step into a previously unknown way of being in the world and found it frightening, but the gift was an awakening to and reconnecting with her deeper Self. Each woman said she needed the wake up call in order to develop spiritually. Each was called to healing and a new life's work that expressed her true self: Elsie was called to develop trust and let go of the control and hyper-vigilance that was killing her. Jana was asked to love herself in order to love others unconditionally, and ultimately fulfill her soul's journey. Rebecca was invited to reconnect with the body from which she'd been so alienated until cancer intervened and called her to reclaim her wholeness.

Many women are stuck in a paradigm shift at midlife. We want the comfort and security of the past even though it doesn't work for us at this stage of life. The feminine life cycle maintains its natural course and will not be thwarted. When it is ignored or denied, you may be blessed with a wake up call that changes everything. Embrace and accept your true self and watch how your physical and mental health blossom.

## CONFLICTS

What keeps women from authenticity? Cultural conditioning is the primary culprit, particularly in the many ways that our culture wounds women. Here are a few ways.

❖ The dualities of our culture devalue the feminine. We are conditioned to believe that there is a split between self and world, body and soul, humans and nature, the rational and the emotional. These splits have created an imbalance between men and women whereby men are valued for their warrior-dominator nature, while women's intuitive, reproductive, relationship-centered nature has been devalued.

❖ There is a lack of support for creative expression, self-nurturing and compassion, and a dishonoring of human sexuality. There is a conflict between domination and reproduction of the species. In other cultures both genders are taught the value of interdependence. For instance, the Native American and all aboriginal cultures revolve around nature and respect for all life, animal and human, as spiritual law.

❖ In a culture that devalues the feminine, the greatest wound is the self-abnegation that prevents a woman from looking within, and instead teaches her to look outside herself for validation. Society says, in the most subtle ways, that we can't have too much power, pleasure or autonomy. Many women spend their entire lives trying to prove they are worthy beings by manifesting the "please disease." This is not healthy. Even if you get all the approval you want, you still won't fill that deep sense of inadequacy. It is by recognizing how you have been bound by culturally imposed self-limiting beliefs that you begin to move forward.

When a woman hears the call to live according to the dictates of her own heart, she may feel it as shameful selfishness. Putting her spiritual growth ahead of obligations to loved ones may seem a rejection of her basic morality. The pull of these seemingly opposed callings not only creates conflict but deep anguish. Because she has been conditioned to doubt her own needs and voice, she is likely to suppress the call of her authentic self and think of it as shameful selfishness. In *The Yang Heart of Yin: On Women's Spiritual Nature*, Wendlyn Alter proposes an unconventional idea when she says, "Perhaps the word selfish must be defined more broadly to mean trapped in the small self." This is an intriguing idea that leads to the need to clarify the notion of "self."

The word self will carry different implications for different women depending how the "small self" is defined. Alter says that the self most women really need to abnegate on the road to spiritual development is the part that needs to please others to generate self-esteem. It is the part that makes nice in order to maintain a comfortable status quo for everyone around us. It is the part that fears change and confrontation. In order to grow spiritually, a woman must cut through the maze of social conditioning and just hang out, all alone in the frightening void where the voice of truth and authenticity can finally be heard. It is this desire to maintain the small self that stunts a woman's spiritual growth and prevents her from claiming her true nature.

When a woman needs to separate herself from loved ones for purposes of authenticity and spiritual growth, she often encounters the obstacle of guilt. Guilt is a product of the conditioned mind. It is the result of an accumulation of shoulds that create conflict over moving forward. Because the urge is to keep the familiar pattern, we often collude in our own betrayal and soon feel despair. Despair comes from alienation from the true self. Alienation occurs when we join with the dark and deny or avoid what we know to be true. Alienation and despair often begin with loss and can precede a descent into the dark night of the soul. Here is an excerpt from my own home-leaving Journal.

*I personally experienced a dreadful alienation for several years before leaving my fifteen-year emotionally abusive relationship. I felt alienated from myself, my community, partner, friends, home, and work—like a glass wall hung between me and the world. What I have learned is that staying in a relationship for so long and ingesting his abusive anger and mood swings in order to keep the peace, resulted in a wall of hatred within me. Containing my hatred and repressed rage generated a sense of helplessness, despair and deep alienation. As hard as I tried to understand my alienation I was unable to see it clearly until I left, thus freeing myself of victimization and regaining my personal power. Only then was I able to take responsibility for seeing and speaking my truth.*

DYNAMICS OF OPPRESSION ∾ Women are filled with beauty, passion and feeling but because of cultural wounding, many are not living authentically and feel victimized. They often see themselves as a reflection of their love relationships. This in itself makes it difficult to separate from harmful relationships. Leaving flies in the face of a woman's relation-centered nature and produces painful inner conflict. Unwillingness to surrender the past in order to heal and grow can often feel like a psychic spasm— a psychological deadlock that really comes from within the woman's own small self. As she tries to balance her conditioning with the call of her authentic self, she becomes deadlocked. If we don't learn the lessons of our relationships they only reappear in the next relationship, because they have to do with us. Here is an excerpt from my Journal three months after I left home.

I don't want to write about abuse. I'm tired of thinking about abuse, mine and others', tired of trying to
understand it. The need to understand puts me right in
the problem, and that means walking all the way through
it. I don't need to understand something that hurts. What
I was doing all those years was trying to figure out why I
hurt, as though something was wrong with me for not
being able to withstand the abuse, for feeling pain
instead. My childhood conditioning taught me that if I felt
pain it meant something wasn't right with me. Rather
than giving myself some nurturing and compassion, or
saying—This hurts, the way you treat me isn't right, it's
not love. Stop what you are doing or I will leave—I
quested to understand why it hurt so much, seeking justi-
fication for both our parts in that long destructive dance
we did together. I should have said, I won't accept this
(fact), it's not going to change (acceptance), confronting
the truth of my pain and his behavior (ending denial),
telling my truth, and leaving (taking action) because
things didn't change (fact). Instead, I retreated into neutral for five years, became one of the living dead. I disen-
gaged emotionally but stayed with the dead body. Dead
bodies produce toxic gas in enclosed places. That's the
poison gas of my dream so long ago. I can still taste my
nausea in that death dream. My crime was choosing to
live with the decaying body of a relationship and swallow
the poison. I tried to live with poison gas just so I could
have a home and relationship . . . a house, not a home,

*an arrangement, not a relationship. I could have died.*
It is easy for an outsider to criticize a woman
who stays in an abusive relationship. Studies on the
physiology of trauma provide insight into such situations. It has been shown that in both mice and
humans, when the nervous system is hyper-aroused
by a situation calling for constant vigilance, any normal person will seek that which is most familiar
regardless of the outcome. In *A Woman's Book of
Life*, Joan Borysenko cites the following example: A
mouse that is locked in a box, given electric shocks,
and then released will return to the box whenever it
is stressed. It seeks safety in familiarity, even if it is
dangerous. The good news is that many women who
have healed from oppression and abuse are called to
careers helping others to heal and grow spiritually—
called back into the box—but this time using their
wisdom and compassion to help others.

Ageism is a particularly insidious form of oppression to which women are more vulnerable than men.
Discrimination based on age is every bit as oppressive
and offensive as discrimination based on sex or race.
Prior to this country's nineteenth century Industrial
Revolution, elders held a place of respect. They were
valued for their role in transmitting tradition, knowledge and wisdom to youth. We now live in a culture
that reveres youth and beauty rather than maturity
and wisdom. Consequently, the forgotten stage of

adult development is that of women aged fifty and beyond. There is virtually no developmental research on this stage of a woman's life. It is as though a woman ceases being a person when her reproductive years end. The truth is that we all have the capacity to develop across the life span, and at midlife a woman can finally feel that she is finding her way home. Why is this? More energy becomes available to her post-menopause. Relieved of reproductive and family responsibility, she is now free to discover who she really is. Inauthentic relationships become harder to abide. There arises an intolerance of limitations placed on us by ourselves and society, of ungrateful loved ones, and of abuse of any sort. This is healthy.

Each woman I interviewed suggested that it is the voice of the heart that leads to authenticity, not the traditional values of our culture that led them to inauthenticity in the first place. The voice that emerged from these women in the privacy of our interviews was that of a long-hidden feminine wisdom that values love, the expression of self-in-relation, and the inner serenity that comes from reclaiming their voice. It is a collective voice of women whose vision is the transformation of self and society, and that recognizes the interconnectedness of all life. When the voice of the heart calls to you, the crossing of a threshold is at hand. Truth is revealed and won't go away. It is up to you to accept the gift and use it to move into authentic, growth-enhancing relationships with yourself and others.

## COURAGE

Change is challenging. When the lowly caterpillar is becoming a butterfly it must endure a period of ambiguity, a time of nothingness, of immense vulnerability. Hanging out in this void can feel like free fall, and requires enormous courage and self-compassion. Courage is synonymous with warriorship. The warrior is someone who is not afraid of empty space, of having no reference points, of vulnerability. I share a passage about free fall from my Journal.

*What am I afraid of? When I sense into this fear I contact bottomless-ness, no ground beneath me. I am in free fall and don't know what the landing will be like. Most often my mind flees to resolution, wanting to create some sort of outcome, not trusting the emptiness. Then body follows mind by constricting ever so slightly in shoulders, arms, gut—as though to protect myself from the impact of the fall. At other times, I feel like a warrior facing battle, loins girded against the unknown, trudging forth into the wilderness with no weapon but my own strength and faith. Yet an unseen hand guides me. My soul reminds me that this time of free fall is rich and valuable. It is time to gather the disparate threads of my life, a life grown rich in diversity and depth because I was always willing to heed the call to live my truth.*

Many women at midlife give birth to the quality of courage. While their bodies go into quiescence and no longer participate in the biological rejuvenation they had experienced monthly since adolescence, a midlife rebirth is reflected outwardly. What was located within for fifty years is now driven to express itself externally as a re-flowering. What flowers is the external manifestation of their ongoing connection to the natural world. They no longer produce eggs and babies, but this same primal energy moves now toward expressing itself at a larger world level. They shed old nurturing roles that kept them physically and emotionally connected at the relationship level. They feel a call to know themselves, perhaps to mother themselves for the first time. Their role as the keeper of life may now express itself toward the environment, peace, social change, or toward ending hunger, war, and violence. Their connection to nature may express itself as a felt need to live in nature, by the sea, on an island, in the wild.

It is at this juncture that a woman may be called to leave home. The urge to connect with herself is primal, yet the boundaries of her current life may be too rigid to flex with her need to grow. She may appear to be in menopausal craziness. Courage in women is often mistaken for insanity. But what is really happening is the same as happens with the seed lying under the fallow winter ground. The life force is

strong enough to push the seedling forth when
nature's cycle so determines. The press to express herself outwardly can only be ignored at great price.

My own mother was unable to permeate the rigid
role boundaries of her life as mother of five children
and wife of a rigid, controlling, hardworking man. At
some midlife point she capitulated to her fears and
poor self-image. She withdrew into a life of despair,
denial and depression. The poignant aspect of this
all-too-common story is that only on her deathbed
did my mother find the courage to speak the truth
about her life. During her final illness my mother
looked up at me with wistful blue eyes and said, "I
took a wrong turn somewhere in my life and don't
know where." My beautiful, intelligent mother was a
victim of both her generation's oppression of women
and her church's bondage of women's bodies. My
mother never knew she had a choice. She didn't
know she could choose to be for her family and for
herself once her physical body was free of child rear-
ing. I can only guess what demons kept my mother in
bondage until death released her at age eighty-one.

Where did my mother take a wrong turn? I
believe it was in not valuing herself, in not knowing
that even after her biological role was fulfilled, life
would continue to call her to a deeper role in relation to the world where her value could expand; in
not realizing that her feminine gifts of sustenance,
intuition and connectedness were not diminished,

and that these gifts were desperately needed in the larger circle of life. My mother took the wrong turn when she chose to abort the growth process inherent in all of life. As the fallow seed must push through the soil to obey its natural destiny, so must women transcend their biology and birth the life force into new form at midlife. Did my mother's stifled life force turn back onto her? I believe it did and that it distorted itself as despair, denial and depression.

We are all lifelong learners if we are willing to hear the challenge of change. The call to reinvent ourselves across the life span requires the courage to look anew at our beliefs and choices. What underlying values might inform how you answer the call to authenticity and how you navigate the midlife journey ahead? What needs reexamination? How might you shed the light of truth on beliefs and values that no longer serve you?

SEEING TRUTH ∾ Every person's worldview expresses some deep truth, and it is wrong only if it claims to possess the whole truth. The truth is there can be your truth, my truth, and our truth. Each of us has the responsibility to discover what is true for ourselves. The primary defenses against seeing truth are avoidance and denial. When we avoid certain issues or people, or when we see things only as we want them to be, we are in denial. In some circles it is politically incorrect to honestly reveal our feelings if those feelings are unpleasant, or to reveal our vulnerability. Beneath the pattern of denial often lies a fear of conflict and the wish to maintain peace at any cost. In deep denial we abandon ourselves completely in order to be accepted and loved.

All life is comprised of polarities: good-bad, light-dark, up-down, in-out, happy-sad. Polarities keep the universe in order. Many people prefer to see only one end of the spectrum of polarities. You may choose to see only the positives and deny the opposites, or vice versa. The reality of polarities can make seeing truth a daunting task. Lily Tomlin once said that all reality is a collective hunch. Examining how you respond to the polarities of life can help to identify your deepest values. When you know your values, choices can be made with greater integrity. Saying yes to what is true for you will definitely move you forward on the path to authenticity. It is one thing to discover your truth, but quite another to live it in the world. It takes courage to confront the inner and outer obstacles to living your truth. Reflecting on your core beliefs can begin the journey into the Self. In his book *Fire in the Belly*, author Sam Keen suggests a series of questions to help uncover your beliefs. These powerful questions can help you see more clearly the truth of your life.

*What do I really want? What brings me joy? Who am I when I dream? Why do I feel the way I do? What do*

*I fear? Who has wounded me? Whom have I injured?*
*How do I deal with guilt? How do I forgive? Whom*
*and what do I love? Who are my people? My family?*
*Where is my place? What is the source of my power?*
*My self-esteem? What is sacred, worthy of respect,*
*inviolable? What are my gifts? What must I do to die*
*with a sense of completeness? What myth have I been*
*living? To what extent are my personal values mere*
*prejudices, and my duties blind commitments to unex-*
*amined norms? What have I sacrificed to win the*
*approval of others? In what ways have I blinded*
*myself, disowned my power, denied my potential?*

Telling our stories is fundamental to the human
search for truth and meaning. With each telling we
reinterpret the past to give meaning to the present.
Each woman I interviewed expressed deep appreciation for being able to tell her story, speak her truth,
and feel heard. They experienced it as healing. For
most it was the first time she'd dared to tell her full
story. The common thread that weaves these women
together is that each had the courage to see her
truth, consciously act upon it, and then enter the
unknown without a map, knowing her life course
would forever be changed.

In a world where truth is a relative concept, how
can you know that you are choosing truth? The answer
lies within you alone. You determine your own truth by
listening to your inner voice, by seeing your life with

fresh eyes, by asking yourself: *what does it mean to be real today?* Nobody can do this for you. Journaling is a safe and effective way to practice personal honesty. The following journaling exercise is adapted from Harriet Cole's book, *Choosing Truth*. Cole suggests you begin by sitting still and creating space to see what the mirror of your life is showing you.

## JOURNALING EXERCISE

❖ Select a time of day to write.

❖ Use a bound book that is both aesthetically appealing and secure, something you can easily carry with you.

❖ Date and describe each entry: place, time, your state of mind, and a picture of the environment that is supporting your journal writing.

❖ Express yourself creatively: sketches, images, color, let the pen follow your course.

❖ Dare to tell the full story. Personal honesty is most important.

❖ Be free. Let your writing flow uncensored from your soul.

❖ Protect your journal, keep it safe. It can be a repository for your deepest truth.

❖ Carve out time to review your writing so you can track your life's evolutions—weekly at first, then quarterly

*The Call Compels the Answer*

FOUR

# *Crossing the Threshold*

*The familiar life horizon has been outgrown;*
*old concepts, ideals, and emotional patterns no longer fit;*
*the time for the passing of a threshold is at hand.*
          —Joseph Campbell *Hero with a Thousand Faces*

What is a threshold? At the mundane level a threshold marks a doorway or an entrance. It is commonly recognized as the place of beginning, the outset. A threshold is also considered a demarcation between two points; it holds the "between space"—often between outside and inside—and can be physical or symbolic. In ancient Greece the threshold was believed to have a dual nature: it was both a barrier and a point of transformation.

At a more sublime level, a threshold can be a metaphorical crossing over to a different place within ourselves—which can feel like a death but can bring new life if we open to it. Writing on the topic of thresholds in *Parabola*, Mircea Eliade defines a threshold as ". . . the limit, the boundary, the frontier that distinguishes and opposes two worlds, and at the same time the paradoxical place where these worlds communicate, where passage from the profane to the sacred world becomes possible." Also in *Parabola*, Thomas Moore states his belief that a threshold ". . . is the true home of creativity . . . also the claustrophobic place of greatest fear," and Joseph Bruhac says that ". . . there is also danger to be found in threshold places, or perhaps the danger is in us, when we come too close to the hub of things, to the intersection where we may cross over, however briefly, and become empowered. When we pass through we may be totally changed."

Change begins with an ending and, if we are to grow, this usually means crossing a threshold—either metaphorically or physically. Staying in lifelong ruts is not our purpose. The task of the second half of life is to reclaim the self we gave up in order to be loved and accepted, when we bought into society's rules (for both men and women). We won't move to a new level of growth until we have let go of the previous

one, and this is particularly true for spiritual growth. Most religions have death-rebirth metaphors suggesting that transformation requires a person to "die" to who she thinks she is before being reborn.
Something does die when there is a major reorientation of consciousness. Our carefully cultivated identity dies and we see a greater truth about who we are. Short or long, the journey usually begins with hearing a call to something deeper. Then as it progresses we enter new experiences, and finally return with new awareness. From fragmentation and emptiness we integrate disparate threads into wholeness.

All life is marked by change and transition. Tribal cultures have traditional rites that mark major life passages. These are rituals to assist members to negotiate normal life changes: birth, coming of age, marriage, elderhood, and death. Rites of passage initiate disengagement from old roles or identities and transition to something new. They provide a way of understanding the natural ending process as well as shedding light on our own inner experience. They also suggest that during times of inner transition a person disengages from the familiar place in society in order to embark on a journey of self-discovery. In the Masai culture, the male goes out into the wilderness alone to find a form of "power" that marks his passage to manhood. During this period of isolation in the wilderness the warrior must cope with fears and aloneness before returning to the tribe to wear his new mantle of manhood. On a mythological level, the male is transformed by moving from inner to outer, by crossing a threshold, hunting and slaying the dragon, and claiming his warrior identity. Love seldom keeps him from pursuing his worldly quest and the good woman waits patiently for his return. Myths express truths that cannot be grasped any other way. The male heroic quest has long been the archetype of the human change process. Masculinity is defined by separation and autonomy. Femininity is defined by connection and relationships. Given these differences, it has only recently been questioned whether male spiritual traditions are appropriate for women's spiritual growth.

In her book *The Spiral Dance*, Starhawk discusses female initiation. She says, "Birth and childhood, of course, are common to all cultures. But our society has not until recently conceptualized the stage of initiation, of personal exploration and self-discovery, as necessary for women. Girls were expected to pass directly from childhood to marriage and motherhood, from control by their fathers to control by their husbands. And initiation demands courage and self-reliance, traits that girls were not encouraged to develop. Today, the stage of initiation may involve establishing a career, exploring relationships, or developing one's creativity. Women who have missed this stage in their youth often find it necessary to go back to it later in life. The later stages of life can only be fully experienced after the initiation is completed and an individualized self has been formed."

How does a woman find power? There are no cultural rites of passage for women, although we do have deep sacred experiences through the physical body and through connection with other women. Childbirth is a rite of passage in the sense that a woman gives birth and then returns to a new role within her family and community. What about women who are unable or choose not to birth a child? What about women who follow the path of career and financial accomplishment, only to find at midlife a longing for something deeper and more meaningful? What about you? There is no road map for a contemporary woman's quest. Once she awakens to her true self and crosses the threshold of change she will find little guidance and much stigma.

While the inner work of spiritual growth is solitary work, we do not have to do it *alone*. The courageous women I interviewed affirmed the immeasurable value of having other women to support them on their journeys. Each woman said she could not have done it without the support of close women friends. Yet the innate feminine relational skill has not been viewed as a strength. Furthermore, the act of answering the call of her authentic self can be perceived as selfishness.

This creates a deep inner conflict if her self-esteem is embedded in the need to please others by maintaining the status quo. That status quo is guarded by the mythical dragon, the slaying of which is the male's prerogative. Women often fear that by challenging the status quo they won't be loved, and precious attachments will be broken. However, I have learned from women's stories that they typically *do* retain their relationships, albeit in a different form, when they leave all that is familiar and loved. This tendency adds a complex and fascinating dimension to the woman's journey.

*Crossing a threshold means moving from believing a woman's life cycle goes from safety pins, hair pins, fraternity pins, clothespins and rolling pins—to believing a woman's life cycle can include any and all possibilities that the world has to offer.*

—Ramona Adams
Crones Counsel IX

ENDINGS ∽ The end is where we start from. Without an ending there is no beginning. William Bridges is a much-admired contemporary expert on life transitions. He has helped many people and organizations cope with life's transitions by providing a road map of the general change process. He acknowledges endings as both opportunity and loss, as well as the way to open new doors. At the very least, endings deprive us of the old, familiar ways of defining ourselves. Bridges identified four different phases of any natural ending. These are disenchantment, disengagement, disidentification, and disorientation.

**Disenchantment** is a process of discovering that the world to which you have become accustomed is no longer "real" and that a significant part of your reality is based on your own misperceptions. Disenchantment occurs when the veils are removed and reality changes, sometimes right before your eyes. There is disillusionment. There may be a loss of dreams or motivation. Take heart, because disenchantment can be a prelude to trading in old realities for new truths—your truths. There will always be guides to help you wake up to new truths; sometimes the guides come in the form of illness, depression, dreams, or a heightened awareness of self-betrayals. Dreams always point to an unconscious truth that is just outside of your awareness.

I had a stunningly clear dream during my own disenchantment phase, but because I did not respond to its message about the reality of my life, the dream revisited me many times. Early in our relationship my partner gave me a lovely ring to symbolize our commitment. The ring held thirty-three matched diamonds totaling one carat. In my recurrent dream, one little diamond would fall out of the setting, roll across the floor, and wedge itself between two floorboards. I was never able to dislodge the diamond from the crack. Each time the dream occurred another diamond was lost, sometimes falling into a toilet, sometimes into slimy mud, always unrecoverable. True disenchantment! Following is an excerpt from my Journal.

*It is hard to say when my own life and spirit began to darken. It got very dark along the way. My home leaving really wasn't sudden or ruthless, as it appeared to some people. It was at least a five-year process, beginning with an insidious disillusionment with all things. I shut down so I would not feel the pain of my reality. I got small, even as I earned my doctorate and became a licensed psychologist. I became a professional helper and lost my own voice. The plotting of my course out of darkness always contained a tiny seed of hope. As the seed germinated over time I had no idea how or when my spirit would flower, but I never doubted that it would. Not to say there was no despair. Despair haunted me regularly, even as the spirit seed struggled toward the light. A part of me trusted the process. I longed to see in the dark. The dark persisted for several years while the seedling took shape, pushed through the dark. Its struggle was heroic in its tenacity, but that is the way with the maturation process. Meanwhile, above the surface, I quietly prepared the soil, enriched it by saving money, kept the path clear by not gathering stones or weeds, by pruning excess branches, and by reaching out. At first the reaching out was in desperation—please save this drowning woman, give her a lifeboat. Learning to accept help took time. Finally, when my despair darkened enough for me to pray for the light to come, when the soil had been prepared sufficiently, when the midwives were engaged, the seedling sprouted and saw the light of day. This seedling had a difficult labor so it knew humility, gratitude and compassion, and can only be open to the light hereafter.*

**Disengagement** is another of the ending phases identified by Bridges. It represents a break in the familiar order of things, a change from how things have always been. The impetus to disengagement comes about in different ways. Sometimes it is forced change created by divorce, being fired from a job, relocation, a broken heart, or death of a loved one. Other times it is a choice, such as following a call to live more authentically. Whenever there is a change in the familiar ways of knowing ourselves there is a meltdown of sorts, grieving is triggered, and maintaining the status quo loses importance.

MARI ∞ Mari revealed the time she realized that all her beliefs and aspirations had turned to ash. "After helping my husband through medical school, I stayed at home for thirteen years raising our three children. Our lives had been defined and determined by the gender roles we had automatically assumed when we married. Over time, interpersonal difficulties became evident: we didn't know how to communicate, deal with feelings, or solve problems. The major turning point happened when I learned that my husband of sixteen years was having an affair. This discovery devastated me. I was angry, and when I expressed it he became angry with me for being angry with him! My husband wouldn't talk about divorce, so I put library books about it on the coffee table trying to start a discussion. There were verbal threats, silences, smashing a glass on the floor. Everything dissolved into nothingness. In total despair, I resolved to leave. After many months of disengagement and preparation, I put the kids and suitcases into the car and we left home.

"Divorce was a rare event in my German culture. Leaving home was a disgrace. Being Catholic made it even more terrible. I was frequently gripped by fear during that period of my life: fear that I would not make it on my own, fear of myself, fear of fear. I had no money, no profession, no self-esteem, and no friends. Something deep inside me knew that I had to leave to save my life! If I didn't I would surely die, but if I did I also might die. It was the hardest thing I've done in my whole life. At the time my life seemed to be coming to an end. In reality, however, an exciting transformation was about to begin."

Without exception, each woman I interviewed expressed a strong belief that she was dying or needed to save her dying soul. In reality, it was that with which she had identified her entire life that was dying. The person she had become wanted to die. The need to cross the threshold became urgent when she actually began to understand this.

**Disidentification** is the inner expression of the outer work of disengagement. It is the loss of familiar ways of thinking about yourself. Old identities stand in the way of change and self-renewal, so the work of disidentification is to loosen the bonds with who you think you are, to let go of how things used to be. This is the beginning of turning inward. I asked Mari what she thought was waiting for her on the other side of her decision to leave home. "It was a death knell. The whole definition of my self was based on my roles of wife and mother. I knew I had to give up the wife part, and then eventually I gave up custody of my three children. I believed then that by giving up these roles and letting go of my identity, I would go 'poof' and vanish into thin air!"

The word identity comes from the Latin meaning *the same*. We live in a culture that teaches that we are our possessions, our looks, our achievements and social status, our personality, our roles. We think these external things mirror who we are and reflect our inherent worth. So we hold on tight. An identity based on externals can never provide true satisfaction or security because when life brings an end to one of these attachments, as it surely does, we suffer.

We suffer because we believe our fabricated self is authentic and its loss feels like a death knell. Buddhist philosophy teaches that all attachment leads to suffering. There is great truth in this because the nature of life is impermanence. Especially today, in this era of high-speed change, the externals holding our lives together can erode in the blink of an eye and identity loss can occur at lightening speed. We cannot know truth and reality if we are attached to things that are destined to change. Staying in deep ruts of attachment to shifting sands actually prevents our awakening. The women who told me their souls were dying also said that the pull to grow was so strong that whatever they risked paled in comparison to the longing to live more authentically.

Three months into my own leaving home journey I was struggling with the emptiness of role loss. A quote from my Journal provides insight into my own dance with disidentification.

*I never know when the dark unnameable distress will come upon me. I go into a foggy emptiness, then a muffled agitation and irritability, feeling so fragile. I want to run off and be someplace else. Unable to focus on a single task, I go round and round, feel worse and worse, irritable, sinking into quicksand. So I ran off to town and spent money, then felt even worse. What nibbles at me right now? I want structure, the familiar security of identity and role. Yes, life without roles is scary. How do I know who I am? I've had roles all my life: daughter, sister, mother, wife, employee, business owner, student, traveler, homemaker, partner, lover, student again, gardener, psychologist, girlfriend, community mediator, homeowner, neighbor. Feeling into these roles and identities I am reminded how stressful they could be at times. I never had time to cultivate and experience empty space. I was frequently on the move to put structure into my life, try on new roles. Now I have none and the space is open for grief to erupt.*

You may find yourself struggling with depression, disorientation and disillusionment all at the same time. You may find yourself needing to consciously disengage from cherished roles before you can move forward. Disidentification is not a static process. We cycle through this phase many times depending on circumstances. It takes as long as it takes, dancing back and forth, both informing and being informed by the need to create an ending before a beginning. As your learned identity dissolves so do the attitudes and outer roles that trap you in the small self. When this happens you know the inner work has begun.

**Disorientation** is the experience of feeling lost and confused, with no future in view. It is a time of nothingness, a kind of underworld. The future is a black abyss. I remember my own experience of disorientation. It seemed to persist unendingly, when in reality it lasted about nine months. I felt completely powerless to make anything happen in my new life, and sitting with the experience of no structure, no purpose, no role and no clear future felt unbearable, if ultimately meaningful. It was an endless, empty, dark place. There was a sense of groundlessness, of disconnection, of not knowing which end was up. I wanted to be able to see in the dark, to know what lay ahead of me, to have a map for the journey. I've since realized that I can drive from California to New York in the dark, using headlights to illuminate only about 150 feet of the road ahead, and still arrive safely.

Elsie said, "At one point my disorientation was so clear I'll never forget it. I recall driving up to my house one day and wondering, 'Where am I? What am I doing here?' I felt like I'd just dropped in from another planet. For a split second a veil was pulled away and I realized that my life as it had been represented only one possible reality. My mind went to thoughts of going crazy. I saw what incredible power I'd given my mind and how limiting that is, yet I didn't know how to change its sole authority over my life." This disorientation phase is a psychic inbetween state. When the old identity has dissolved, when the terrain is murky and there are no maps of the unfamiliar territory ahead, what do we do? Being in that gap is so disorienting. Yet it is in that desolate neutral zone that the voice of truth is heard. The growth comes from staying aware of the gap and embracing the silence of the unknown.

What is required of us during disorientation is an important element of spiritual growth. When things fall apart we are faced with the limits of our ability to control. The urge is to grab onto something that feels solid. Whenever we go outside the box of our familiar identity, old patterns will resurface trying to restore solidity to what feels like groundlessness. The real growth of transition lies in allowing the emptiness of this rich, barren in-between place that Bridges calls the "neutral zone." The work in the neutral zone is to surrender, to give in to the disorientation and emptiness, not run away from it. There will be voices, both inner and outer, telling you what you should do to end the darkness, how to take control. These anxious voices must be silenced in order for you to hear your true inner voice. Although it is challenging to sustain, there are spiritual riches in the work of surrender.

Connie described the emptiness of the neutral zone when she said, "It feels like being stuck, like waiting, looking out on a calm ocean waiting for a wave that doesn't arrive. Being on an empty street corner waiting for a bus, not knowing when it will come or where it will take me. I also dread the road ahead and fear not being in control. Then sometimes I'm excited about not knowing the outcome. At times I experience pure freedom and happiness at knowing I'm in this place and don't have to do anything, don't have to make decisions, just trust the process. Sometimes there is no emotion at all. Sitting with this emptiness has been the biggest lesson of my life." Bridges confirms Connie's experience when he says, "The neutral zone provides access to an angle of vision on life that one can get nowhere else. And it is a succession of such views over a lifetime that produces wisdom." May we all grow in wisdom.

The ending phases defined by Bridges—disengagement, disidentification, disenchantment and disorientation—provide valuable tools for making sense of what can be a chaotic experience. They are normal parts of the human change process and should not be aborted out of fear. It is important to recognize that these ending phases seldom arise in neatly defined intervals. They often occur simultaneously, may or may not be clearly defined, and you may cycle through one or more phases several times. As a whole, Bridges' phases characterize a descent into some dark and unfamiliar aspects of your self.

## THE NATURE OF DESCENT

Whenever we cross a threshold into uncharted territory, there is a descent into the unknown. Sometimes this is referred to as the dark night of the soul, a journey to the underworld, or meeting the dark goddess. Often it feels like depression.

Mythology has immortalized the descents of famous goddesses such as Demeter, Persephone and Inanna, and these myths provide the contemporary woman with an understanding of her own descent. In the descent a woman is stripped of familiar ways of knowing herself, her identity dissolves, and there is no map of the terrain. The road ahead is obscured while the road behind has disappeared. She is required to go deeply inward to find guidance. This means relying on her inner knowing, reclaiming her feelings, and trusting that at the end of the dark journey lies the potential to meet her authentic self. It is by conscious surrender to the descent, by going *through* it rather than around it, that transformation occurs. In this sense, descent is a true initiation of the midlife woman's soul.

The crossing of a midlife threshold marks a passage to a different place for a woman. The archetypal male hero's journey is characterized by going alone into the physical world, slaying a dragon of sorts, and acquiring new powers. As such, the male spiritual quest is not a useful model for the woman's spiritual journey. The difference is that when a woman responds to the call of her authentic self she crosses a threshold (either physically or metaphorically) and goes deeply inward, rather than outward. She descends *into* herself in order to do battle with the inner demons that have kept her locked in her small self. Hers is not the immortalized hero's journey! As she pursues her journey she is often mystified, misunderstood and stigmatized by loved ones and society. She does not have to do it alone, for there are comrades on the path waiting to support her growth.

Take some time to consider the endings you have experienced in your life. What symbols marked those endings? What helped you through the scary places? How did you make meaning of your endings? What followed your endings?

FIVE

# Shadows in the Call

*We forget*
*that everything we know now*
*was once unknown.*

—Kati Pressman

A critical part of a midlife woman's spiritual journey is the willingness to not know where she is
headed, to trust far beyond her understanding and
perhaps her tolerance, and to meet the scary places
within. This is why we need to hear other women's
stories—to know we are not crazy or bad, that we are
part of the collective feminine journey, and that we
can trust ourselves. Women's stories are an important

medium for reclaiming authentic voice. Stories help a woman to value her strengths and to understand the roots of her despair. It is through stories that the collective feminine experience is shared. Even if we don't have all the answers, we can share the questions and provide inspiration and support to those who dare to make the journey. Women have been locked in silence for too long, but that is changing. Hearing other women's stories and telling your own lets you know you are connected to the larger story of women's experience.

## SHADOW SIDE: MEETING THE SCARY PLACES

Inside each of us and usually hidden until midlife (or forever) is a shadow side. Shadow typically refers to a part of our self that is only partially illuminated because it is blocked by the belief that the personality is who we really are. Carl Jung coined the term shadow to refer to the darker aspects of ourselves which contribute unknowingly to the creation of a false self. The shadow is a mixture of traits and attitudes that the conscious mind wants to reject or disown, the unwanted parts of ourselves we have relegated to the unconscious level. These are the places that scare us.

It is the shadow side that emerges at midlife and upsets the proverbial apple cart of our lives. Just when we think we have it all together personally, professionally and relationship-wise, the shadow emerges and we encounter all kinds of new experiences. Meeting the shadow at midlife will shatter your identity, but it also offers the promise of renewal and wholeness. Your shadow is the door to growth and integration. A confrontation with the shadow can be frightening and is generally frowned upon by society. It is comforting to know, however, that this is a normal part of the journey to authentic self and you are not losing your mind, as Elsie thought. There is gold in your shadow if you can trust yourself to fully embrace it.

EMOTIONAL TRAPS: OBSTACLES ON THE PATH

Emotional traps will show up as part of your shadow side. These are the ways you sabotage yourself when the familiar has slipped away, either because you have physically left home or because your inner search has taken you beyond the familiar into uncharted territory. Growth and expansion are your natural birthright. Emotional traps serve to keep you trapped in the small self. Awakening is the process of waking up *from* these unconscious patterns and *into* your true nature. To become spiritually awake you need to understand how you are actually sabotaging the natural process of your own spiritual growth. The following is from my Journal almost a year into my home-leaving journey.

My leaving home journey began as a long-overdue birthing process. The labor pains were felt initially as a combination of excitement, fear and willingness to meet the unknown. Busy with preparation of endings and new beginnings, what to keep, what to let go. For a while the excitement of newness, of release from the old and painful, carried me into the future, buoyed me up, distracted me. Pure momentum itself distracts, much as the "engine" of childbirth produces unstoppable energy that overrides the pain. There are new experiences, a different sense of self in new surroundings, choices to be made, and the exhilarating freedom to be myself and be for myself. There are also shadows here.

Somewhere in this process I became aware of my emotional dependency on those friends who had midwifed my leap into the unknown. Just as with any growth process, we must ultimately stand on our own two feet as supportive others let go of our hand and wish us well. This feels like a major turning point. I must face myself in new ways with the realization that I am alone, on my own at a stage of life when my peers are settling into retirement, enjoying the fruits of their labor. Facing myself on an unknown road to somewhere is scary. Where is the road map? How do I know my choices when I can't see the road? And the loneliness of aloneness. What to do with the emotions that accompany aloneness at the stage of life when my body is changing, my energy isn't what it used to be, when familiar aspects *of my life have been left behind, and difficult choices are faced daily?*

Emotional traps are your vulnerable places. Having deliberately removed yourself from familiar supports and patterns, emotional vulnerabilities are certain to surface with a vengeance. If you are prone to dependency, this vulnerability will be magnified here. If you tend toward ambivalence, then difficulty making choices and commitment will most certainly present itself at every opportunity. If you are prone to self-doubt and self-criticism, these obstacles will bedevil you in your loneliest, most groundless moments. Emotional traps await each woman who has made it this far into the journey.

When you feel you can no longer keep moving ahead by yourself as you deal with your vulnerable places, it may be time to get into therapy. When you're really stuck, a compassionate professional can guide and support you. A year into my home-leaving journey I was beset by doubts, fears, anxiety, depression and insomnia. Truly stuck, I could see nothing but darkness on the road ahead. I experienced extended states of limbo. "When is something going to happen?" I asked myself. In my deepest despair I began psychotherapy. In our third session the therapist said to me, "Ani, I notice that you see yourself as powerless." That feedback hit me squarely between the eyes and woke me up in a hurry. I had never seen myself as powerless, yet I was firmly stuck in the belief that I was powerless. As I worked in therapy with my feeling of powerlessness, my life began to move forward.

There are probably as many emotional traps as there are personality types. I know of three that are universal, and have discovered that women who embark on the journey to authentic self are particularly vulnerable to these obstacles. These traps are your inner critic, loneliness and fear.

INNER CRITIC ∞ The inner critic is known by several names, including the inner judge, the censor, the gremlin, and the superego. This is the part of you that blames, criticizes, judges, condemns and compares unmercifully. It is the part of you that wants the safety of the known. The inner critic is what you will face when familiar boundaries and structures are left behind. The mind wants to protect you from the dark gaping hole of the unknown, wants to do something about it, find security and familiarity in old identity and behavior patterns. The inner critic acts whenever it recognizes something of which it disapproves. Long-buried shame can rear its ugly head, berating you with feelings of worthlessness, of wanting to hide because you feel so deficient. Shame and guilt almost never arise except in response to self-judgment. As a function of the inner critic, shame is an emotion with a strong physiological and cognitive component. It is also the feeling component of the inner voice that says you are somehow flawed. Shame rears its ugly head during the transition journey because we have left behind much of our former personae—those roles and relationships that daily affirm who and how we are have now been relinquished.

Our culture is replete with messages and images of the contented, secure and vibrantly healthy older woman securely attached to an equally secure and handsome husband, heading into their golden years of freedom and financial security, with or without Viagra. The inner critic frightens you and causes anxiety because it is an emotional attack, a judgment, a form of self-betrayal that keeps egging you on to reach some illusory perfect image, never letting you rest or feel okay about yourself. This is from my Journal:

*I've left behind my professional role, my home and neighborhood, my community of friends, the familiar routines that were securely rooted in my idea of myself. Opening to the emptiness of limbo is frightening and exhausting. My inner critic tells me that I will be a bag lady forever with nobody to take care of me in my old age. It is during these dark hours that I feel shame for not conforming to society's and family's image of the well-educated, successful, professional woman.*

If you attune yourself to your self-judging
process, you will hear an ever-present voice speaking
familiar phrases. You will recognize these "tapes" as
what you heard while growing up—standards, ideals,
warnings, parental reprimands and restrictions from
childhood. These voices were internalized, swallowed
whole at an early age, and became part of your reality as though they were truth. The truth is that each
is a form of emotional blackmail aimed at preventing
you from living an authentic peaceful life. If you
expand or feel too good the critic will provide you
with a dose of reality. It will never accept you, appreciate you, or acknowledge your pain. The inner critic
is one of the main sources of personal suffering, and
it inflicts damage by maintaining low self-esteem,
guilt, shame and self-recrimination. Besides the pervasive personal suffering it causes, the inner critic
can easily halt your inner journey. More from my
Journal of that time.

*And then it was moving day. I was aware of want-
ing to reach out and touch him. I did once, caressed his
face out of love. There was a flicker of openness in his
eyes, then retreat. So we went about our task of disman-
tling our home, moving my belongings into storage. Then
the moment of parting came. We hugged and said good-
bye. I was completely present with the feel of his body
next to mine. I let it in along with the memories of us, of
a life together. And then he was gone in a flash. Grief*

*erupted. It welled up from my soul. I was wracked by
tears and sobs as the walls came tumbling down. Pure
grief for all I was losing, all I had to leave to call back my
spirit, to regain myself. I was utterly alone in that
wretched storage unit on a forlorn back road on the foggy
coast of central California. The enormity of my aloneness came crashing down on me. I sat in that storage bin
surrounded by a bunch of material possessions, most of
which I'd dragged around with me for thirty years, and
thought this was all there was left of me—a bunch of
material junk.*

*The wailing seemed to begin in my bones, maybe my
soul. Part of me wondered where that awful sound was
coming from. At first I didn't know it was my wailing, it
seemed so far away. It washed in waves over my body . . .
keening, someone later said. I was grieving for my home,
my sense of belonging, and my place in the universe of
humankind. Words can't adequately describe the sensation of hitting bottom in that moment. A dark chasm
opened up and I fell in, fell into muffled darkness. There
was no place to go, nothing to hang onto, no person to
reach out to. The experience of utter aloneness engulfed
me. Yes, I am now alone. It hit me squarely in my solar
plexus, a thud of reality. Oh, the groundlessness of that
reality. I was at that moment a homeless woman.*

*In that vulnerable moment of utter groundlessness,
my inner critic rushed in. The first voice was one of
regret: "I've made a horrible mistake by leaving. I've lost*

too much. *I do not recognize value.*" *I heard the word value repeatedly:* "*I'm stupid not to see the value I've left behind. I've never had the ability to recognize value. I'll never recoup the valuable situation I've left. I've made another wretched life mistake, one that is unredeemable. I'm doomed to this aloneness until I die . . . and that will be soon.*

My inner critic berated me mercilessly during my most vulnerable moment. In reality, my leaving was a profound act of valuing me, reclaiming my spirit, being compassionate toward myself, an act of self-care. Yet my inner critic reached its ugly hand into a crack in my self-esteem and took unfair advantage of my vulnerability, causing deep doubt, fear, and hopelessness, and it had the potential to sabotage my journey.

### EXERCISE

You can begin to understand the power behind your inner critic by learning to observe yourself closely as you experience an attack. This is difficult to do because your critic always remains just out of your awareness. For instance, you may have a shame attack after being laid off from a job. You might be feeling unworthy or tell yourself you will never make it on your own, that you are doomed to be a bag lady. Fear and shame can paralyze you, undermine your self-esteem, and you may not even notice it is happening. What is required here is staying aware of your thoughts, bodily sensations, feelings, and a curiosity to be open to what you find. Do not engage the shame attack. As you notice the feelings and thoughts provoked by the attack, you can speak them aloud, write them down, or list them silently to yourself. With practice you will become more aware of your inner critic and more skillfully disengage from its attacks.

Another way of working with the inner critic is to sit with a friend who will reflect your self-judgment(s) back to you. For instance, you may put yourself down repeatedly for your weight, skin, or a feature of your body. Your friend will calmly speak back to you (without malice) the judgment you have about yourself. She will then listen quietly as you explore your reaction. You may react with sadness, shame, humor, or a buried childhood memory might arise and you feel twelve years old again. You can also audio tape yourself delivering a familiar self-attack several times, then play it back once and stop while you explore it privately. Repeat the attack as many times as you need to in order to contact as deeply as possible the effect it has on you. You will learn a lot about your shadow side!

LONELINESS ∾ Aloneness is a primal state of being. It is what we started out with. On the other hand, loneliness is an acquired state of mind. It is a product of dependency. Loneliness is rooted in the wish to be attached somewhere, to someone, to an identity, so you don't have to feel the original aloneness. At its core, loneliness is a longing to reconnect with true home. The difference between aloneness and loneliness lies in the connection to the higher self. The capacity to be alone and content with solitude is possible when there is both an inner connection and the willingness to be present, without judgment, with your feelings, needs and behaviors.

Elsie counsels, "I want other women to know that their journey doesn't have to look like anyone else's. And to choose a few traveling companions who will be absolutely nonjudgmental and not try to control you into societal structures. Our companions need not get nervous about us, just accept us. And there are times when you feel so alone you can't stand it. But it has to be this way because nobody else can go through it with you. I never knew I could be so lonely. But that's because of always focusing outside my self. When I learn to love myself and when I know myself as God, how can I be lonely? I know loneliness comes from being out of touch with my essential nature."

We don't want to feel what we feel because it is uncomfortable and can bring up despair and hope-lessness. We want relief from the anxiety of loneli-ness, want to make it wrong, assign blame, make it go away—anything to avoid the in-between place of transition. Pema Chodron is a Buddhist nun and author of *When Things Fall Apart.* Chodron encour-ages us to resist reacting to discomfort and to culti-vate openness to what is. She calls this the middle way, having an open mind that is comfortable with paradox and ambiguity. The middle way is difficult because it goes against our habitual grain of seeking a quick fix to discomfort. When we can open to what is present in each moment, we will be more comfort-able with loneliness.

Chodron teaches us several ways of working with loneliness. The first is having less desire to change our loneliness. When desire to escape lone-liness can be subdued and seen for the emotional trap that it is, the restlessness shifts. The second response is contentment. When we are content with what we have there is less fear, more accept-ance, and fewer beliefs that erasing loneliness will bring happiness. Another is ceasing activity whose purpose is to escape from being alone with our-selves. This means not looking for outer-directed ways to comfort ourselves—food, drink, activity, people. Another is the practice of presence. This means becoming aware of how things are in the present moment. The nice thing about the discipline of presence is that it will always open us to the truth of our authentic self.

SOPHIA.∾.Sophia is a sixty-year-old woman who has taken many risks for the sake of living more authentically. She speaks poignantly of the unresolved remnants of her loneliness. "For me, loneliness is felt as a lack of meaningful connection with other human beings, the times I feel there is nobody who recognizes, or sees, or is available to engage the real me. It's the haunting feeling that sometimes arises that I have to do everything for myself, that I'm alone in the world. Maybe it's archetypal. Loneliness is now less circumstantial than it is existential. It just IS. My comfort with aloneness abates loneliness. It's a life skill I have developed on this path that I'm more comfortable being alone than ever before, so loneliness is less of an issue. I have more resources, more ways to find solace than previously. I am less rigid and controlling about my circumstances because I am more trusting of life, so I can now allow more into my life. It is a new comfort level even though circumstances seem so uncertain."

Looking at loneliness honestly and without old reactive patterns allows us to see more clearly just who we are. Loneliness is not a threat or a punishment to be fixed. It just is! Chodron suggests that when loneliness and alienation visit us we can view the experience as a valuable opportunity to relax and be open to what is . . . to choose what she calls the middle way.

FEAR ✑ We all experience fear as we grow toward authenticity. What are you afraid of? Fear of change, of making decisions, of being vulnerable or inadequate? Or of being adequate just as you are? Fear of losing connections to relationships, of going into the unknown? What resonates in your heart when you feel fear? What is needed? You cannot change something you don't recognize. In simple terms, this is how the cycle of fear works in all human beings.

1. Something triggers a fearful thought ("I'll never be loved again," "I can't make it on my own").

2. Anxiety kicks in and your body begins to produce adrenaline.

3. Elevated adrenaline creates physical symptoms such as increased heart rate, light- headedness, and sweaty palms.

4. Your mind notices the physical symptoms and generates more fearful thoughts ("I'll be a bag lady," "I'll spend the rest of my life alone").

5. These new fearful thoughts cause your adrenaline level to increase even more, producing stronger physical symptoms, perhaps heart palpitations, nausea, or racing thoughts.

6. As these physical symptoms escalate, your mind generates ever-stronger fearful thoughts ("What if I never get unstuck?" "What if I get sick and die alone?").

In their wonderful book *Repacking Your Bags*, Leider and Shapiro identify what they call the four deadly fears. It is by meeting, embracing and accepting each of these fears that we can achieve a more authentic life. The first fear is that of having lived a meaningless life. Our roles in the world, the work we do and the prescribed responsibilities associated with it, can keep us from living a meaningful life. This is what the midlife women whose stories inform this book meant when they said: "My spirit had died," "My soul was dying," "I had to save my own life." When a woman hears the call to a more authentic life, she must face the choices inherent in giving up prescribed roles and then find the courage to live a more meaningful life.

The second fear is that of being alone. We can spend a lifetime searching for love, but true love remains out of reach until we are unafraid to be alone and befriend our authentic self. You will remember, from the earlier section on loneliness, that the capacity to be alone is an outgrowth of an inner connection with self and the willingness to be present with your deepest feelings, needs and reactions.

The third fear is of being lost. This fear ties many

women to a place, both literally and figuratively. Gail Collins in *America's Women* says, "The history of American women is all about leaving home, crossing oceans and continents, getting jobs, living on their own . . . the center of our story is the tension between the yearning to create a home and the urge to get out of it." Who really knows where she belongs until she's been away from it? Being lost allows a woman the freedom to find herself. Once connected with her authenticity, she can now create a true sense of place that allows her to no longer feel lost. This is what Elsie meant when she said: "The home had to go because the mantle of responsibility never left me, day or night. I hate that kind of living, it's nuts, yet it's painfully wrenching to give up my images of what home used to mean. I don't yet know what home is. I do know I must first establish home within myself."

The fourth deadly fear identified by Leider and Shapiro, is the fear of death. This fear always underlies the call to more fully live the life we have been given.

CATHY ∞ Cathy was forty years old and married, with a young daughter, when she left home to follow a call to the ministry. She was feeling dissatisfied in her marriage and it was a time of personal exploration that her husband supported. She saw it as running away from home and was thrilled because it gave her the freedom to pursue a calling after so many years of stultifying marriage.

Cathy said "I became conscious of being alive after a long childhood illness. My serious heart defect was corrected at age sixteen and this gave me a new physical life. Having been given the gift of life, I knew I couldn't spend it living unhappily like my mother did. 'How am I to spend this life?' has always been a guiding question for me. Twenty years later it continues to propel me. I am content in the ministry. It's a good match for me, and I am always growing."

WORKING WITH FEAR ∽ If you wait for fear to disappear, trust me, it won't. There are two approaches to fear. One is leaning *away* from fear and the other is leaning *into* fear. The first approach says that your mind is the starting point for fear, so it's important to take charge of your thoughts. This is the cognitive psychology approach of shifting the focus away from fearful thoughts to positive ones. It is a method for harnessing the power of the mind and controlling negative thoughts by doing something to purge them from the mind: inspirational readings, avoiding anxiety-provoking situations, thought stopping and thought substitution, avoiding vulnerable moments. For instance, you might develop a mantra to use as soon as fear arises. You can repeat a phrase such as, "I am stronger than my fear." When you are in an emotionally vulnerable state, fear is heightened. In addition, you are more vulnerable to fearful thoughts when tired, hungry or lonely. Be sensitive to your most vulnerable times and do something to nurture yourself. The emphasis of the cognitive approach to working with fear is on the *mind* and on *doing* something to change the thoughts and situations that give rise to fear.

The second approach to working with fear is quite different. It comes from the ancient Eastern spiritual philosophies that ask us to feel the fear fully and, as with any emotion, to accept and open to it, letting the fear soften us rather than hardening and resisting it. When we resist and harden to feelings we create aversion, a kind of armoring, and eventually isolation and emptiness. The willingness to actively engage with fear means leaning *in* to it rather than leaning *away* from it. It does not mean losing your balance or getting lost. It means embracing what is.

When we lean in to fear, we contact directly the tight sensation in the throat, heart or belly that is fear's expression in the body. When facing fear by contacting bodily sensations, what often happens is that the mind immediately produces a story, often based on prior experiences. The key is to recognize fear thoughts for what they are and connect with the bodily experience of fear. This is because the mind and body are connected. For instance, my 43-year old patient who was a childhood incest victim still experiences a terrifying adrenaline rush whenever she sees a car like her father's drive past her house. Victims of trauma can heal from the cycle of fear reactivation by repeatedly grounding themselves in their bodies and their physical environment, which brings them into the present reality rather than the painful past. This is no simple task. It needs to be practiced over and over, yet being in the present is the key to freedom from the prison of fear, self-judgment, and anxiety.

Some people are highly skilled at controlling their minds, but do not necessarily have the capacity to tolerate emotions, especially in the face of fear. Others who are not practiced in controlling their thoughts and are ruled by emotions can benefit from consciously shifting the focus away from fearful thoughts to positive ones. Still other people are disconnected from their bodily sensations and miss out on a universe of information about being human. A hallmark of spiritual growth is developing a balance between thoughts, feelings and bodily sensations, and being comfortable with each as it is appropriate to the situation. Working with fear is challenging and requires compassion, the capacity to open your heart to what is.

## COMPASSION, CHOICE, COMPROMISE

COMPASSION ∾ Compassion is a direct antidote to the obstacles presented by your inner critic, loneliness and fear. It is a quality of the heart that allows you to

be more open to the truth of what is, without judgment. Compassion is the ability to feel loving kindness in the presence of difficult feelings and situations.
It is not pity. It is the willingness to move toward
whatever scares you without contracting in aversion.
If you are not able to acknowledge or be with your
inner experience, it will be hard to feel compassion for
yourself. In my work as a therapist I've noticed that
people more easily feel compassion for others than for
themselves. This is because your inner judge criticizes
you for feeling kindly toward yourself. It says "Stop
pitying yourself," or "You don't deserve kindness," or
"Buck up, that's for softies and sissies." The more inner
critic you have, the more self-compassion is required.
Compassion is opening to difficult feelings—ours or
another's. When we know and accept our own shadow
side we can be present with the darkness of others.
From my Journal:

*What I really needed was protection and nurturing
from a compassionate inner mother. When my helper
friends mobilized to midwife my home leaving, I finally got
the protective mother I needed. They gave me validation,
caring and protection, a safe place in which to rest, the
gift of a lifetime. They filled the deep hole that couldn't be
filled by me because I had no model for self-compassion.
Now I do! Now I can treat myself with loving kindness,
can care for myself like a good mother would—with
strength and compassion.*

Cultivating compassion can dissolve barriers and end alienation, isolation, judgment, fear and loneliness. Self-compassion means consciously making choices that will sustain you in your transition and beyond. It can open your heart to courage, self-nurturing, forgiveness and joy. Lasting change occurs when we trust ourselves as a source of compassion and wisdom. One Valentine's Day a woman friend sent me the following ritual to honor ourselves as women. It speaks to the self-compassion that is difficult or elusive for so many women and teaches that when we open our hearts to ourselves we can be more accepting of others.

*Imagine* a woman who accepts herself. A woman who descends into her own richly textured humanity, turning a merciful eye toward all she discovers. Whose capacity to live without judgment toward others deepens as she is merciful toward herself.

*Imagine* a woman who turns toward herself with interest and attention. A woman who acknowledges her own feelings, thoughts and perceptions. Whose capacity to be available to others deepens as she is available to herself.

*Imagine* a woman who fully participates in her own life. A woman who meets each blessing with gratitude and each challenge with creativity. Whose capacity to participate in her relationships

deepens as she participates in her own life.
**Imagine** a woman who remains faithful to herself
through all the seasons of life. A woman who pre-
serves allegiance to herself even in the face of
opposition. Whose capacity to sustain interest in
others deepens as she is loyal to herself.
**Imagine** yourself as this woman.

CHOICE ∞ Do you think you will be punished if
you become authentic? If so, try to look honestly at
your god-concept and beliefs on external authority.
Who holds power and authority over you? As a
midlife woman, to whom do you answer? Many
women are terrified of making choices. We don't
know if a choice is wise or wrong until we've made it
and then lived it out. Choices present themselves
throughout life, and if we don't choose, somebody
else will usually do it for us. The reality of being
human is that because we live in a web of relationships, choice does not occur without loss. This is
hard stuff, particularly for women who are so embedded in relationships. The family used to be the
beginning and end of a woman's life. Many women
saw their mothers as unhappy and decided early on
that they didn't want that. This has propelled many
women's choices. We have choices in all areas of life,
including what we hold onto and what we let go of.

Sophia describes her struggle with the choices
she has made. "There are lots of built-in threats once

we step out of the norm. Husbands can't make sense of us. Our children vacillate between admiration, respect, fear and disapproval. My twenty-something daughter said: 'I don't know what to be enthusiastic about any more for you.' Validation and encouragement from loved ones often take the form of 'don't change.' This may not be active antagonism to what I am doing, but it is an implied message of disapproval. From where I stand my choices have their own internal meaning and learning. They have all the elements of risk, growth and commitment. I've done a lot of compromise in my choice making in order not to alienate myself from my children and parents. As a member of the sandwich generation, it was easy with my spouse compared to with my children and parents."

The *sandwich generation* (to which many contemporary midlife women belong) describes those who are sandwiched between children who still need them and aging parents who now need their care. The family of women—daughters and daughters-in-law—does most of the care taking of elderly parents. As people live longer there will be more aging parents needing our care. To whom does a woman talk about her dilemma around painful choices when sandwiched between disapproving loved ones? How does she live with integrity and still make life-enhancing choices?

Sophia continues, "Looking back, I would not have made the choice to be so readily available to my children and parents. I took a huge step when I sold the family home and gave up maintaining a home base for my adult children. They let me know they wished they had a Mom who kept a home for them. My kids would be okay with my not coming home for Christmas only if I had a good excuse—like being in the Peace Corps in Africa! I've always compromised myself for the sake of family values and this remains a difficult area to reconcile. I am in the process of changing my personal values around holidays and family obligations. In the eyes of my loved ones it makes me more of a black sheep than a courageous woman."

It takes a huge amount of courage for you to follow the call to authenticity. There are so many pressures to stay in the mold, so many ramifications of choice. A lot of women who bought the package of wife, caretaker, and compromiser were sorely disappointed. This is often a source of depression, self-medication and anger. You don't want to acknowledge that you only got half the pie, and there is often a family-societal backlash when you choose to pursue your own needs. The stigma encountered from family, society and contemporaries is a terrific counterforce to following your heart. Taking risks at this stage of life requires a basic trust in your self and in the goodness of life. It is especially poignant when you are looking at the downhill side of life and there is a natural desire to have someone to be there for you. If you are alienating loved ones by choosing for yourself, it can feel like burning beloved bridges.

Sophia talks honestly about this dark side of the journey. "It's a process I continue to stumble my way through. We haven't talked about the organic process of moving into the second half of life, the very fact that we haven't the same energy level, want to be contemplative, to go within, the reality of having to support ourselves—the fear that is practically built into our DNA about becoming a bag lady. The challenges to the body of living on the edge are different now than they were ten years ago. Maintaining healthy disciplines are especially challenged by constant change, very high stress and uncertainty, along with expecting positive performance from ourselves. Those of us who leave home at this stage of life are dealing with higher levels of loss, change, highs, lows—all those measures of stress. For those with major health issues I suppose leaving home can be part of the cure by living fully in the face of fear. That's the stuff of heroines!"

We need a solid base within ourselves to cope with the ups and downs of choice and compromise, to tolerate the fear, to enter into the unknown. Most spiritual traditions say the tools are within and that our authentic self can be trusted. Yet as women we are working against heavy odds because *what* we know and *how* we know has largely been conditioned out of us. Many women are frightened of making choices because choosing authenticity involves sacrifice, or because they are afraid of being wrong. If we are unwilling to take the risk, we can end up losing a great deal more—our integrity, our health, our soul. Unconscious choice is how women end up living other people's lives. Conscious choice is a creative act, the heart of authenticity. One woman said, "I like thinking that my choices make the path appear in front of me. Trying to plan for something six steps ahead is ridiculous because there are so many choices to be made between the present and the future."

COMPROMISE ∞ The art of compromise is a necessary part of life, and women tend to be better at it than men. Too often, compromise means that everyone gets what nobody wants! Janet was recently widowed when I interviewed her. She was proud of the long career as an unpaid political activist that she carved out for herself while successfully raising three children. She reflected on the role of compromise in her long marriage to a well-known international scientist. "Our compromises didn't meet either of our needs, but it was better than the alternative for each of us. What I regretted most when my husband died was that we'd long ago lost the closeness of early marriage. We became good friends, kept our emotional distance, found satisfaction in work. We didn't ask each other very many questions. The emotional distance grew over the years. We stopped arguing, trying to explain or understand, quite early on. We both learned to settle for less." Janet wrote this poem at midlife and shares it here because it speaks poignantly of the costs of her compromises.

*The sun is bright on the grass, but I cannot feel it.*
*The air is cold, the lilac without perfume.*
*The lovers talk as they pass. I cannot hear them . . .*
*I sit in the world as if in an empty room.*

*A memory stirs. The air is heavy with fragrance.*
*I am a child again, walking in wind and rain.*
*I taste the cold drops on my tongue. The birds are silent,*
*I am close to the world . . . its loveliness is pain.*

*Beyond the window, children shout at play.*
*What have I lost? And where along the way?*

Yes, there are shadows in any midlife call to awaken. We are asked to face our shadow . . . those largely unexamined aspects of our personality, our vulnerable places. Confronting the scary places might bring up self-judgment, loneliness and fear—emotional traps that can sabotage our inner journey. There are ways to work with these and other obstacles on our path, including cultivating compassion. Compassion for ourselves is a direct antidote to our fears, loneliness and self-judgments. Compassion toward others can dissolve the alienation and isolation that often visit those of us who travel this path. Embarking on the midlife journey to authenticity will bring us face to face with the need to find a balance between autonomy, wholeness, and the powerful need for meaningful personal relationships. The road to authentic self will throw us into the unmapped territory of changing roles and shifting values that require choice, compromise and compassion at all levels.

## EXERCISE

CULTIVATING COMPASSION

The Dali Lama offers a simple practice that will increase your capacity for compassion.

Spend a few minutes at the beginning of each day remembering that we all want the same things (to be happy, to be loved) and that we are all connected to one another.

Spend five minutes—breathing in, cherishing you; breathing out, cherishing others. If you think about a person you have difficulty cherishing, extend your loving kindness to them anyway. During the day, extend that attitude to everyone you meet. Practice cherishing the simplest person (clerks, attendants, as well as the other people in your life). Cherish the people you love and those you dislike.

Continue this practice until it becomes easy and natural for you

SIX

# Keys to Conscious Living

*We learn to trust by taking risks.*
*What if not trusting is the bigger risk?*

—Kati Pressman

Y ou have within you the potential for becoming
more conscious. Most spiritual traditions teach
practices for deepening awareness and increasing
consciousness as a way to grow spiritually. These
practices include meditation, prayer, and a variety of
ways of being still, being open, and paying attention. Increasing consciousness involves a shift in
perception about your potential and possible realities. It is a creative act we are all capable of. Once

you've experienced it, you know it. In the first half of life growth is equated with gaining more: more height, personality, knowledge, education, achievement, money. Most of the growth in the second half of life has the look and feel of loss. Change, challenge and choice speak meaningful messages at midlife. When listened to, these messages will take you to a new level of consciousness that is equivalent to spiritual growth.

## TRANSITION AS SPIRITUAL GROWTH

Transition seldom reveals its full meaning. It is an opportunity to listen deeply to your inner voice, to awaken, to see things differently, to ask new questions, to live more fully. When in the throes of transition its importance is seldom recognized until you get down the road a bit and can see that you have moved through a level of transformation. The gift of a midlife call is that you are asked to work through many layers of obsolete emotional patterns, in particular the soul work of loss, grief, letting go, guilt and forgiveness.

LOSS ∾ Loss is always a wake up call. Its message is that time is finite, that life can't be taken for granted, that you cannot remain a slave to another's expectations. Loss never leaves you where it finds you. It changes you deeply, makes room for you to grow. Through loss you can open to something new.

Sometimes what is lost is a sense of control. Loss of control can be liberating when it is used as an opportunity to befriend the emptiness and the spaciousness within, and to appreciate the deeper meaning of your life.

The vulnerability in loss teaches about love and compassion as few lessons can. At age twenty-six, I lost my beloved two-year-old son. He died suddenly in a hospital emergency room in the dark of a foggy coastal New England night. I was devastated and changed forever. A parent never heals from the loss of a child, but eventually finds a place within to hold the loss so she can go forward with life. My earliest awareness of the change wrought on me by loss occurred about four months after my child's death. On a cold wintry night I dragged myself to my first post-loss social event, my best girlfriend's house wares party. I felt raw and vulnerable as I mingled with the other guests, as though I had no skin. It took my best effort to keep my emotional head above water that night. The party began with an icebreaker game to write on a slip of paper one thing you want most. Then around the circle each woman read aloud what she wanted: new house, dishwasher, better job, another child. My feelings of vulnerability increased dramatically as my turn came and I shared what I most wanted: an end to the killing in Viet Nam. There was a palpable silence during which I felt stripped bare, turned inside out, bleeding. At that moment I knew I was different from my peers. The memory still breaks my heart. I would never again be the same person. I had crossed a threshold to a place most people don't experience. I was different inside. And that was the beginning of my search for wholeness and meaning through many years of spiritual exploration and growth.

That long-ago house wares party experience reflected to me the knowledge that my soul-wrenching loss had stripped the veils from my eyes, stolen my trust and innocence, and catapulted me to a new level of consciousness. Loss opens a huge window of awareness through which we can see with new eyes. It is a humbling experience from which we are given the spiritual gifts of love, compassion, acceptance and letting go.

GRIEF ∞ Loss is an inevitable part of being human and we must grieve our losses. Grief and loss are well known to most women by midlife. We grieve the loss of youth, children leaving home, our diminishing energy, the loss of loved ones, and perhaps our lessening health. A woman will be called upon to grieve further losses when she heeds the call of her authentic self: the familiar structure of her life and relationships; a customary security, role and status; innocence and blind faith; and too often the approval and support of loved ones. Most of all, she will grieve the parts of herself that have been buried for so long. Grief is a quiet thing. It is a process that takes as much time as it needs. Give yourself the time you need to heal your emotional wounds just as you do a physical wound. Don't postpone, deny, cover, or run from your grief as this can complicate the natural healing process. It is essential to feel your feelings, embrace your fear and pain, and know that the only way out is through.

When my child died so suddenly I was inconsolable, but numb inside. I had come from a good, solid, working class family that didn't give much credence to feelings. We didn't talk about our feelings or ourselves. Therefore, I had no outlet for my feelings and the normal grief process became stuck and unresolved for me. Sixteen years later during Gestalt Therapy training at Esalen Institute, my teacher remarked that I seemed to be seeing life through a filter of loss. Indeed, I did have many fears and anxieties, never felt safe, and was hyper-vigilant to the point of exhaustion, always waiting for the next trauma to strike. My teacher invited me to use that session to say good-bye to my lost child. I gathered all my courage and began the work. I felt that I was falling into a deep, dark, endless pit of pain. In the presence of each moment, there was no place to hide. The potency of my unresolved grief was so intense I had to let go, to surrender to it. The intensity of the experience filtered through every cell of my body. Afterwards, I was almost comatose, unable to move my limbs or speak for almost an hour. The first thing I noticed was how bright the sunshine was, how blue the sky, how green the grass. It was a moment of pure grace. Moving through the remnants of my grief after so many years hiding from it gave me back my life, touched something essential within, and liberated me.

Next to the death of a loved one, facing the end of a relationship is probably one of the most painful experiences we endure. If the path you've chosen leads to the end of a relationship, be gentle with yourself during this transition. You can't make someone else follow along on your spiritual journey. Having the support of a few good friends who know how to really listen is invaluable. Being able to talk through your loss is an especially significant aspect of the grieving and letting go process. Be patient with yourself.

Grief is an inevitable part of this journey. In fact, embarking on a spiritual path can be one long process of grieving, accepting, and letting go. This is because in grief we are forced to a level of feeling that is usually below our threshold of awareness, beyond the personality level, touching something essential in our being. The heart is cracked open. And we are somehow closer to the authentic self.

LETTING GO ∽ It is a universal truth that we must let go before we can move forward. Kayla is a

Jewish woman who had a near-death experience after an auto accident and then experienced a profound awakening. She came out of the hospital after a year-long recovery and found she'd lost every material possession she owned, as well as her marriage and children. She said, "What helped me most with loss and letting go was finally realizing that there is no story about it, it happened, it's gone. I can't even make up a story; it's all in the past, done. What is more important is to not give any meaning to losing my house, my kids and everything. That's how my life has been. I think I've got something and it's gone. Nothing is permanent. Such a tough lesson for me."

In the journey to authenticity, precious gifts are received. Yet these same gifts can be calling you away. Life has a way of shocking us into seeing our attachments and grasping patterns. What do you need to let go of? Your identity, roles or relationships? Hopes and dreams? Are you a woman who equates the word attachment with "caring," or the word detachment with "not caring?" If so, you are not alone. The human heart is tricky. At a subconscious level I believed that if I didn't hang onto my grief it meant I didn't care about my lost child. I caused myself untold suffering and deprived myself of precious gifts. I am so grateful to be free from the burden of grief.

Mari left home when such behavior was an unforgivable act. Her advice about letting go? "You let go of things over the course of your life, or you get a crash course later on." This includes letting go of the person you used to be, of the past and things that are connected to your past, particularly thoughts and feelings such as anger, resentment and guilt. Sometimes letting go is about giving up attachment to being right or to being an injured innocent. What are you holding onto from your past that prevents you from moving forward?

A powerful way to let go of the past is to perform some kind of releasing ritual. A week before our interview Ann performed an outdoor ceremony for releasing her wedding vows. "I knew instinctually that because I am a person who keeps my word, my thirty year old marriage vows were holding me back. That morning I cried a lot, keened, howled, as I realized how huge this un-vowing ceremony was." She invited close woman friends, and together they assembled candles, ashes, rose petals, her husband's picture, their wedding album, and a letter to him declaring "who I am now." The women were invited to let spirit work through them. Ann told Jim all that she liked about their life together; she wore a black scarf like a widow, and truly experienced the death. Each woman performed a part of the letting go ceremony: they anointed Ann, gave her a beautiful new scarf, splashed her with lavender, sang to her, danced, caressed her, loved her. And she let it all in, to her surprise.

Letting go is the fruit of learning to surrender to and accept life's inevitable losses. The more we can accept and appreciate what is, the less focus there is on what is gone. We accept by seeing clearly what is true and holding it with kindness, eventually coming to peace with it, as Ann did. There are many things we each have to accept: ourselves, aging, death, our feelings, change, failure, success, our body, the unknown, universal truths. You probably have others to add to this list. Something is lost, yet something is gained when you can let go and love what is.

GUILT ∞ Have you identified your personal barriers to letting go? These may include the inner critic, fear, and a host of unresolved emotional traps. For women, the most common emotional obstacle to letting go is guilt. Guilt is the unconscious belief that you are somehow doing something bad or wrong. It is a thought pattern to which you may be particularly vulnerable if guilt was used in your childhood to abuse or punish you. The bad thing about guilt is that it always prevents you from making choices that can improve the quality of your life. Like facing and letting go of fear, you can loosen its grip on you by recognizing and owning your guilt. Your guilt is your guilt, it belongs only to you, and is often a product of low self-esteem. When you value the needs of others over your own needs, your self-esteem suffers. This creates a vicious cycle: the less you value yourself, the less you value your own needs, and the more susceptible you are to guilt.

Jana said, "Physically leaving home was imperative for me. I needed space for myself even though we owned a large, gorgeous house. I couldn't find myself without being alone. It was not about loss as much as about retrieving myself. I had immense guilt about telling my family I was leaving home. I thought I was disrupting their lives, or that they wouldn't understand. They were shocked, but still loved me. I've been so afraid of disappointing people. I've lived my whole life pleasing others."

Facing guilt head on is like fighting for your life. The first step is to become aware of when guilt is influencing your choices. Instead of waiting for illness, burnout, or an emotional crisis, accept that some initial fear and discomfort is normal. Find a trusted friend or a psychotherapist to help you to take full responsibility for your guilt. Take small steps toward making guilt-free choices. It's a small price to pay for living more authentically.

FORGIVENESS ∞ The question of forgiveness is something humans will debate until the end of time. What makes forgiveness different from passive acceptance? From giving in? Forgiveness is not always about justice, but can be about accountability. Do we need to let go before we can forgive, or forgive before we can let go? Or are they the same?

How is letting go different from letting be? We certainly need to grieve before we can either heal or forgive. But what are the elements of forgiveness? Voncille, Jacquie, Ann and Phyllis provide us with personal insights into the role of forgiveness in their home-leaving journey.

VONCILLE ∽ At age fifty-nine, Voncille found herself with an adult son and teenage twins, and a dependent, emotionally needy husband of thirty-three years. She said, "My soul was dying, I could not stay. There were so many questions of why I had made decisions for everyone but myself." Like so many women who had cared for others all their adult lives, she was called to slow down and get to know herself on the inside. Voncille moved into her one-room art studio. She describes the loneliness and isolation as visceral. "I felt so different, so weird, so misunderstood. I was scared of the outcome, afraid I would never want to go back, worried about how much time it could take to learn to be myself, to feel good in my own skin."

I asked Voncille if forgiveness of self or another was an issue. "Yes! Forgiveness of myself, and accepting my right to take time for healing and honoring all that I am. Also, forgiveness of my husband for being *who* and *how* he is. I've handled the relationship by letting go of criticism and judgment, while simultaneously realizing I do have choice to go or

stay. This was a major aspect of the shift toward forgiveness and acceptance of what is."

At age fifty-seven, Jacquie (introduced in chapter
1) found that, "In order to live and breathe I could
not continue to live in the same space with my husband of thirty-two years." She understood that part-
nership is a two-way street and took responsibility for
her part in the relationship dysfunction. She didn't
want a divorce. She wanted to agree on how to live
together as equal partners in mutual respect. He didn't
see where disrespect existed, but Jacquie did. So she
needed space where she could be authentic, could
learn how to confront disrespect in the moment.
Before leaving home Jacquie worked on forgiveness.
She wanted her next step to be made without resentment or guilt.

After she left, Jacquie and her husband continued a more formal relationship by maintaining weekly contact through their Sunday brunch ritual. On
the first Father's Day in thirty-five years that Jacquie
wasn't with her husband, he died suddenly on the
ninth hole of a golf course. Does Jacquie regret leaving home? "I am totally joyful I did the work of forgiveness, let go of resentment, and didn't carry guilt
into my home leaving. I did it all with kindness and
compassion, which allowed joy into the process of
saying the final good-byes, selling our house, and
now moving into the future."

Ann (also intoduce in chapter 1) is a woman for whom the leaving home process has been long, slow, with honest grieving; she didn't run away or fill herself up with busyness. She was terrified by the deep loneliness she experienced. She explained, "To me forgiveness is seeing the truth and accepting it. The hard thing about becoming conscious is that you become really pissed off when you see things as they are. Yet seeing is a relative thing. We have choices about how to see things: blame him, blame myself, or see both ways and hold them in balance. If we can see the truth about another and accept it, great. That is an element of forgiveness.

"Forgiveness of myself has been the biggest thing. I felt so much guilt. The big challenge was to know and accept my own value, and appreciate my husband's value instead of judging and blaming him. Forgiveness comes when I take full responsibility for my life instead of blaming anyone else for the life I'm not living. The good thing about living alone is that when your stuff comes up you know it's yours. The more I love and accept myself, the more I live authentically; the more I live authentically the more I accept myself. I now see that everything is perfect as it has been—and there is nothing else to forgive. I got there because I gave myself the freedom to be me. That is true liberation."

Forgiveness may be the most difficult work you

ever do. It also promises the greatest rewards.
Forgiveness is a tricky subject. It is an inner release,
not an outer act. To forgive means to give up one way
of thinking for a higher way of thinking, and recognizing that you don't know the whole story. We judge
whatever we don't understand, and by judging others
we are really judging ourselves. To forgive doesn't
mean you condone bad behavior, or are required to
reconcile, nor does it mean giving in. It is a decision
to not carry the burden of anger any longer, to release
it, to choose freedom from toxic pain. It is really a gift
we give ourselves . . . when we are ready.

PHYLLIS ∞ Phyllis lost her teen-age son in a car
accident shortly after she divorced his father and had
remarried. She went through a profound and painful
transformation that almost took her life. Suffering a
crisis of major depression, she actually had to be
spoon fed at one point. I asked Phyllis about the role
of forgiveness in her healing journey. She described a
stripping down process that was catalyzed by her
deep loss.

"Forgiveness is *the* issue! All that I had accumulated over my lifetime had to come to an end in
order for me to free myself of my pain. I had to
cleanse my soul, mind, and body of anger and hatred
through forgiveness. All those things were being pro-
jected onto others, along with the projection of my
true self. This was a huge barrier. A tool I used to

heal was to go back through my life and forgive everybody I felt had wronged me, and to forgive myself for all the mistakes I'd made and about which I carried a lot of guilt. I had to forgive my former husband. It was easy to forgive everyone else but him. I'm still working on it. I have very little anger at this point. What happened has happened. It had to happen for me to find my own purpose and inner peace. Had it not happened I'm not sure I'd have what I have today. This inner peace! It's unlike anything I could have imagined. I'm not a religious person, but I believe in a higher power and am very spiritual. I believe that in my depths of despair the Holy Spirit reached out, took my hand and said 'get up.' And I did. She held me tight while I recovered. My recovery took me beyond anything I could imagine. It took me deep within and once I'd rid myself of the soot stuck in all the crevices of my heart my authentic self was revealed. I've always been me but I didn't know it, because so many of my life experiences were like a cloud covering the genuine me. I now feel free, whole, good."

Both Ann and Phyllis learned that forgiveness has to do with letting go of judgments of self and others. It is the release of pain and suffering that makes it possible for healing and acceptance to begin. Forgiveness restores right relationship with self and others so you can find wholeness, balance and peace. Being in right relationship means to live your values with integrity and coherence; to discern, act and speak your inner truth; to own your shadow side; and take responsibility for your own actions. There is ample evidence from mind-body research that forgiveness benefits the body, that it improves the immune system and makes a big difference to your general health. There is a strong relationship between self-forgiveness and healing depression and certain forms of cancer. Forgiveness of self and others is a prerequisite to healing at the emotional, physical and spiritual levels.

All true change is made from self-acceptance, which suggests that self-forgiveness is a prelude to forgiving another. Self-forgiveness requires thinking through one's actions, taking responsibility for them, and opening your heart to yourself. I asked Phyllis what she found when she went deep within. "I found lots of anger, frustration, pain and long-held grudges. I also realized that I'd had many bad experiences in my life, and that most of these were of my own doing and my responsibility entirely. I had to cleanse myself of everything I was carrying inside that was painful. I knew I was ready and all my past searching had brought me to this new understanding at age fifty-one."

Phyllis created a healing ritual that brought about self-forgiveness. "Each day I'd close my eyes, go inside, and imagine something peaceful. The Holy

Spirit I believe, created the image that always sur-
faced. It was an image of a lake, trees, and a peaceful
and beautiful place. The lake was filled with holy
water. I could see the back of me, naked, just skin
and bones, walking into the lake. When I'd submerge
myself in this wonderful warm liquid I'd become part
of it. If there was any darkness lodged in my mind,
body or soul—it would disappear in the water. Each
time I did this meditation, I came out of the water
stronger, healthier, more pure, peaceful, powerful and
compassionate. Because things have a way of slipping
back into the mind, this is a self-forgiveness meditation that I still do each day."

The self is developed in childhood partly in relationship to others, making us relational beings. You
can't have sound relationships with others if you are
not right with yourself and have not owned your
repressed shadow side. In your work on forgiveness, it
is helpful to inquire into your ideas about "God." We
invent our God ideas in the image of our parents.
People with low self-esteem tend to see God as puni-
tive, while those with high self-esteem have God
images that are loving and forgiving. What is your
image of a God figure: loving and forgiving, or puni-
tive and unforgiving?

To forgive is a big, brave step toward authenticity. It lightens your burden, frees your pain, and opens
the door to your real self. It may also feel like a risk.

When you are ready to risk and trust the emergent process, the old shell breaks apart and you move to a new level. This is the great spiritual gift that is yours when you embark on the path to authentic self.

## EXERCISE

If there is someone you are ready to forgive, you might want to try the following forgiveness ritual. Feel free to make your own modifications.

Set aside some time for yourself in a quiet, private setting. Allow the image of the person you want to forgive to come into your mind and speak the following affirmation aloud: "I freely and fully forgive (name the person). I completely let go of the issue/person that has hurt me. I cast off my burden of resentment, it is finished forever. I wish you well from this day forward. We are both set free." Offer thanks and go on with your day. The person/situation will certainly cross your mind again, so simply repeat: "I release this person and this situation," and dismiss the thought. You will find that the memory returns less and less. Soon you'll be free of it forever.

## STEPPING STONES TO SELF

What makes it so difficult to be deeply authentic, to feel free to be who we naturally are? Most spiritual traditions attribute this difficulty to a case of mistaken identity. We are identified with a self-concept—certain ideas and images that we think represent who we are—that greatly limits our experience of our self and the world. This is the personality—a conglomeration of emotional and thought patterns, mixed with a unique biological wiring, that forms a self-concept and usually determines our relationship to the world. The personality has many faces. We can be one person at work, another at home, another in the bedroom, another while walking in nature. How are we to know which is real? Is there really a separate self? This is a tricky topic that requires some understanding of the "self versus no-self" ideas that distinguish Western and Eastern philosophies.

The concept of self has been wrestled with in all spiritual traditions, as well as within Western psychological schools of thought such as humanism, existentialism and transpersonal psychology. From a psychological perspective, when our sense of self is stable, real, positive and congruent, we experience a greater sense of self-worth. We are said to be inner-directed, rather than outer-directed. There is no need for external trappings to shore up a false self when our desires and actions reflect who and what we are. Eastern philosophies such as Hinduism and Buddhism teach that seeing through the belief in a separate self is the key to true happiness, and that letting go of ideas of self is the way to personal liberation. Generally the term *self* is used to represent the small self, and *Self* signifies the higher self. The small self is the personality, the ego, or the false self we present to the world. We create suffering for ourselves when we identify with the personality because the small self is identified with externals that will inevitably change: the body, relationships, health, age, success, failure, control, home, job, beliefs and so on.

The concept of Self is much more vast because it embodies a higher level of consciousness. The Self is our authentic nature, our essential Beingness that has been obscured by the inevitable development of the personality and living according to societal rules and roles. This is what each woman I interviewed was suffering when she blurted out, "My soul was dying," "I couldn't find myself anymore, " or "My spirit had died," as her reason for leaving home. Human nature yearns for something larger than self. It yearns for Self. The sacred Hindu text, the *Bhagavad-Gita*, says it well in chapter 6, verse 5:

> *Lift up the self by the Self*
> *And don't let the self droop down,*
> *For the Self is the self's only friend*
> *And the self is the Self's only foe.*

TRUST AND COMMITMENT ∽ Transition is never a linear process. There is always a natural movement of expansion and contraction—the heart opens and

the heart closes, there are fallow periods of emptiness and not knowing. It is not always obvious what
home means to each of us, when we need to leave
it, or how. How do we know all will be well? We
don't. Whenever we head into the unknown, hidden fears and self-doubts loom up, the analytic mind
takes over and says the risk is too great. Don't beat
yourself up with criticism and blame. This is where
commitment becomes important. Commitment is a
choice. It has to do with doing what feels right at
the heart level and not letting the mind talk you out
of it. To be committed is to have a passion and a
loyalty to something you really believe in, to walk
your talk, and to keep your attention open to what
calls you. It means looking for possible clues or signals about the path on which you are to travel. It
means trusting the natural flow of life, being open to
the next step, and taking that step when the
moment seems right.

There is no person, no outer authority you can
trust to guide you. But if you listen to what calls you,
to the silent yearning in your heart, you can trust life
to support risk-taking. Support always shows up
when we act with integrity and commitment to living more authentically. Some commitments are nurtured when people have hit bottom, when strength-
ened by fire. Once a commitment is made and you've
put all your resources behind it, things can move

very quickly. All sorts of unseen forces will manifest in the direction of your commitment.

Sophia generously shared her thoughts on trust and commitment. She said, "It helps me to think of the entire leaving home journey and its shifting of values as a trust walk. Each new step I take builds a foundation for trust in my values. When I've listened to my inner guidance, trust has been validated for me. Ultimately, I have returned to a basic trust in myself rather than in the cultural messages about how life works. Trust in myself needs to be balanced by trust in a larger co-creative energy. Then we see we are not creating all by ourselves. I've learned that I am part of a whole that is safe and supportive. I do my part and I'm supported. This works for me at this stage of my life. It was hard won because I didn't grow up with an ideology to hold onto. I needed to create it for myself." How does trust feed into letting go of attachments, expectations, control and self-image? How do we find the fine line between how much to trust, how much to control? If the door doesn't open, how much is our responsibility to push on it, versus relaxing into the idea that it wasn't meant to open? These are issues a woman must face continuously as she makes choices and compromises.

I asked Sophia what she is committing to on a trust walk. What about commitment to a higher Self? She responded, "In my early life, commitment

was equated with martyrdom. I'd commit to something and saw no other choice but to go forward. I
now know that my choice is how I respond to a situation. There is no room for martyrdom on this journey. A strong motivator for me has been 'Where can
I serve?' Then the question emerges, 'What about
service to my higher Self?' I find no fulfillment in
simply doing things to serve the little me, the personality me. I've known for some time that I'm committed to transformation of consciousness. I believe I
have a part to play in this, but all I can understand is
I need to transform my own consciousness, then I am
an instrument of transformation. The choices I've
encountered on my own journey have taught me to
do my part. I feel a need to offer service—whether
through a job, expressing an idea, or a service to the
whole—something I'm drawn to give. And in the
process something in me shifts."

Whenever you enter the unknown and surrender
to deep knowing, you are likely to cross a threshold
into new territory of difficult choices and compromises. You are asked to draw on inner resources you
didn't know you had. It has been said that we cannot
discover new oceans unless we have the courage to
lose sight of the shore. In surrendering to your intuitive knowing you find that your experience is not an
enemy, but your teacher and something to embrace.
The urge to control your experience causes you to

miss so many growth opportunities. Trusting your
experience enables you to hear your authentic voice.
Listen and honor it, even the mistakes.

Sophia suggests that midlife asks you to look
back on your life and take stock of your relationship
to commitment. Have your commitments been based
in martyrdom? Were there thresholds where you had
to take a stand? Was your commitment what you
would have liked it to be? If not, can you identify the
emotional traps that got in the way? Do you know
how to listen to your inner voice and allow it to
guide your choices and commitments? Can you let go
enough to trust the deep knowing that will help you
when you don't know how to navigate the road
ahead? Can you risk surrendering to the unknown, to
lose sight of the shore? Take some time to think of
the stepping-stones of your life, those key times that
were powerful or difficult. What were the gifts, the
keys to your becoming more authentic?

There are many paths to spiritual growth, but
the leaving home journey is perhaps unique to
women's spiritual growth. It is a spiritual journey
because it can bring you to the same awakening that
ancient spiritual practices teach. In order for the
journey to be sustainable—for a woman to go all the
way through it and resurface with the gift of her
authentic self—a specific line of travel is asked of
her. It calls for a willingness to commit to the whole,

to the unknown, and to the unknowable—and trust the call to awaken in this life.

In Phase III feminine spirituality is explored from both historical and contemporary perspectives. The perennial spiritual practices of stillness and openness are offered as vital resources to sustain a descent into the unknowns of your journey. Finally, practical tools for managing the everyday rigors of work, relationships, parenting and playing are offered.

*Tools for the Journey*

# SEVEN

## Women's Spirituality

*I am*
*all the things*
*I wanted to know*
*about myself*
*and was afraid to ask.*

—Kati Pressman

Amerivan women's lives have changed dramatically in the last half-century. This is because feminism's "first wave" opened doors for women to education, social justice, equality and freedom of choice.
There followed a tremendous increase in longevity
due to unprecedented medical and technological

advances. Statistically speaking, if a woman today lives to be sixty-five she can expect to live another nineteen years, until age eighty-four. In the last thirty years alone, women have gained earning power, economic and political clout, and leadership opportunities that are changing the world. This same feminist movement that so enhanced contemporary women's lives did not address women's spirituality, not wanting to detract from the pressing work of social change. Today the patriarchal religious values of sexism, oppression, and aggression remain perennial problems for women everywhere.

This last decade has been a turning point, a time when the critical mass of female energy necessary for further social transformation has blossomed. As we entered the twenty-first century, nineteen million baby boomer women were entering menopause. Many of these women were active in the feminist movement of the last three decades, and they are now redefining themselves spiritually. Around age fifty, most women begin to free themselves from cultural constraints to become less defined by others and more by their own needs and choices. Along with this huge swell in the numbers of midlife women has come a burgeoning interest in ancient and contemporary forms of women's spirituality, conscious aging, and the ancient wisdom traditions. For the first time in more than three thousand years, we

are hearing women's voices on matters of religion
and spirituality.

This trend is part of a larger cultural shift that
social researcher Paul Ray calls the *integral culture*.
Ray's research has identified a subculture of forty-four
million people, or 24 percent of the American adult
population, whose values center on spirituality, self-
actualization, self-expression, ecology, and elevation
of the feminine to a new place in recent human history. This subculture is comprised of twice as many
women as men. It is deeply concerned with reinte-
gration of what has been fragmented by modernism:
self, authenticity, connection with community and
nature, and tolerance for diverse views and traditions. According to Ray's research, this subculture is
not a fringe phenomenon, but is very much a part of
mainstream American life.

## THE FOURTH WAVE

This new activist movement, feminism's "fourth
wave," is gathering women across all faiths. The first
wave of feminism fought for women's suffrage. The
second wave accomplished legal and economic gains.
Along came the third-wave feminists, women in
their twenties and thirties who embraced women's
rights along with an individualism that celebrated
sexual freedom, men, the gay culture, and clothes.
The long-awaited fourth wave of spiritually informed

activists began in response to global violence and a
politically conservative environment. But it seems
that the critical energizing event was 9/11. The
emphasis is on connecting women through national
gatherings that affirm and support women's bonds
across religious, cultural and ethnic borders. It is a
fusion of universal spirituality with social justice that
focuses on wider issues than individualism and personal spirituality. Power is redefined with respect to
those values critical to healing poverty, violence at
home, and war—such values as tolerance, reverence
for nature, mutuality, and cooperation. The fourth
wave is a new kind of political activism, the heart of
which is women's spirituality.

## WHY A WOMEN'S SPIRITUALITY?

Women's spirituality is blossoming again. As history is rewritten by contemporary archeological find-
ings and by modern women scholars like Riane Eisler
and Marija Gimbutas, we learn that the elemental
power of the female was the focus of ancient cultures
as far back as could be traced. Artifacts related to the
religion of the Goddess date back as early as 25,000
B.C. Furthermore, these Goddess cultures were
peaceful and earth-centered societies, without
weapons or defensive structures. The Goddess has
always been a metaphor for the divine, and for
today's women she exemplifies the ancient feminine

heritage that was eradicated by the rise of a Judeo-Christian religion beginning around 1800 B.C. The Goddess is returning because she provides contemporary women with the self-concept of strength, wholeness, and freedom. Images of Goddesses such as Kali, Isis, Artemis and Aphrodite are a source of healing and validation that supports women taking responsibility for their own lives. The Goddess symbolizes the holistic nature of life, the connection of all beings, and the power of the female body and mind. Women are intrinsically mystical, valuing intuition, dreams and symbolism, and many have found that the ancient rituals of earth-centered religions honor these qualities. For many contemporary women the Goddess symbolizes the spiritual power to challenge institutions of oppression and to create new, life-sustaining cultures. For a more in-depth look at the history of women's spirituality, I recommend Charlene Spretnak's classic book *The Politics of Women's Spirituality*.

Spirituality is connection. A woman generally connects with others fairly easily. Yet her spiritual challenge is to connect first with herself, then with the larger community. Women everywhere have experienced a profound loss by being cut off from their feminine values by the dominant patriarchal religions. There is deep suffering in a woman once she recognizes this disconnection that is akin to a

death of the soul. In times past, there was no avenue
for us to even speak of this loss. We have a long history of being oppressed, the worst examples of which
are epitomized by the Burning Times of the sixteenth
and seventeenth centuries. An estimated nine million women were tortured or burned to death simply
for their feminine values and powers, for aligning
with the forces of nature. The woman killings of the
Burning Times led to profound emotional and spiritual isolation and distrust. For many centuries thereafter women had no avenues for spiritual expression
except through patriarchal religions, which were
devised by men and taught the subordination of
women. These rigid and narrowly defined religions
lacked decision-making roles for women and were
closed to alternative paths for exploring one's spiritual nature. Until recently, when a woman left the
patriarchy behind there was nothing to turn to
because there was no non-patriarchal form of spirituality for women to choose. The earliest feminist writ-
ings were devalued and mostly absent from literature.
It was like stepping into a dark and frightening abyss
if a woman dared to follow the call of her spirit.
Elinor Gadon, author of *The Once and Future
Goddess*, offers this concise view of women's history:
"In the beginning was the Goddess. The patriarchy
suppressed her power. But the Goddess is re-awaken-
ing just as we need her most."

The hard edges of contemporary life and cultural conditioning continue to suppress a woman's ability to connect with her feminine power. Yet with the courage and support to risk change, every woman can reclaim her elemental wholeness. Remember Karen who, at age sixty-two, felt like a non-person after years of living through the lives of loved ones? Karen had long felt a push from within to shed her old roles and be more authentic, yet nobody took her needs seriously. She had always been passionate about the earth and describes herself as an "ecologist in neon letters." She longed to live more from her core values, but alas had no role models. So Karen joined a younger woman's group and watched and learned. She experimented with Native American rituals, Goddess ceremony, metaphysics, song, dance and alternative healers. Like so many women who embrace feminine spirituality, Karen was able to reclaim her self-image of strength, wholeness and expanding personal power. Karen's story helps us realize that mentors can come from any age group. As a woman grows spiritually she becomes more earth and community-oriented, she reaches out to heal the iniquities caused by social injustice, racism, and discrimination. She naturally becomes involved in something larger than her small self.

NATURE ∞ Many of the courageous women I interviewed expressed a passion for nature, an urgent need to touch the earth, a reverence for all things wild and free and natural. They passionately dig into the soil, feel its richness and depth, and work with earth in luxurious and sensual ways. Phyllis spoke reverently of her own precious earth project as a labyrinth-like creation that can be seen from every window of her little house, sensuously curved paths meandering through her oak mini-forest, lovely stones artfully lining her pathways. She noted with enormous pride that she spends every free minute working in her earth, shaping and reshaping it, luxuriating in the freedom, creativity and strength she finds there.

As I pondered what this pattern might be, I realized that it is the midlife woman's way of outwardly expressing that which has existed hidden within her body during the first half of life, during her fertile years. It is a naturally occurring midlife biological phenomenon, affirms medical scientist Joan Borysenko. By our very nature we are elemental, deeply connected to and influenced by natural rhythms of the moon, the seasons, and thereby the earth. When our biological nature is transformed at menopause, where does that energy of nature go? It doesn't die. It is transformed by the normal changes our body undergoes at midlife. Like the seasons, a woman's outer life reflects the natural order of things. Autumn is a time of shedding: green turns to brown, once verdant trees become bare as leaves dry up and fall away. The vibrancy of spring and summer has been shed. Earth appears barren and brown, devoid of life, color and energy. The fields lie fallow, resting, waiting, and gathering energy for their next phase of life.

While her body goes into quiescence and does not re-seed itself as we see repeated in nature's seasons, a midlife woman's rebirth is reflected outwardly. What was located within for fifty years is now expressed in new ways. What occurs is an external expression of her continued connection to the natural world. She no longer produces eggs and babies, but this same energy expresses itself on a larger level. She sheds old nurturing roles that kept her physically and emotionally secured. She feels a call to know herself, maybe to mother herself for the first time. Her role as the keeper of life expands to the larger world, and typically toward the environment, peace, social change, and natural processes that have gone awry because of human kind's greed and violence.

When a midlife woman tells me about her passion for nature and wild things, I know her inner biological force is moving out to the wider circle of life. Nurturing and connection may look different in these women, but in reality this is a natural extension of her feminine nature. Her connection to Mother Earth may manifest as a felt need to live in nature, by the sea, on an island, in wildness. It is at this juncture that a woman may leave home. The urge to connect with her larger self is urgently felt. The boundaries of her current life may be too rigid to flex with her primal need to grow. To others she appears to be in a midlife crisis or some sort of menopausal craziness. But it is the same as the wintering bulb sleeping beneath the fallow earth: when the life force is strong enough, it will push the seedling forth in accordance with nature's law. And so it is with many midlife women. The press to express can only be contained at great price. The eternal energy of nature will not be thwarted.

Women everywhere are reclaiming ancient forms of spiritual expression because there is a longing for the feminine in religion and in our lives. *Megatrends for Women* by Patricia Aburdene refers to the contemporary re-emergence of the Goddess as, ". . . a movement that defies theology, reinterprets archeology, and transforms his story into hers." Megatrends estimates that this movement in the United States alone involves about a half million people, and many more are quietly incorporating Goddess theology into their lives through readings and personal worship. Goddess spirituality is not necessarily the same as women's spirituality. Women's spirituality is a multi-disciplinary, fertile, unstructured wave of creative, intellectual and spiritual activity. It embraces multiple ways of acknowledging and expressing feminine sources of wisdom and harmony.

Following is a sample of the ancient and contemporary expressions of women's spirituality that are blossoming today. They each have at their core a reverence for the earth, nature and balance.

ENVIRONMENTALISM

*Ecopsychology* is an emerging wing of the environmental movement that is spearheaded by women. It has to do with human behavior toward the earth. Ecopsychologists are motivated by a deep concern for life and all that is natural. They argue that our sanity is grounded in the natural world, that the current ecological crisis signifies a pathological estrangement from nature, and that there must be a psychological reconciliation with the earth and all living things. The planet's environmental health is directly related to the mental health of its inhabitants. The work of ecopsycholgy is to re-examine our idea of sanity in this materialistic, growth-oriented culture and to heal Earth and its inhabitants by raising public awareness of the relationship between human behavior and environmental destruction. According to most estimates, the developed world represents 22 percent of the global population, yet consumes 70 to 85 percent of its resources and produces 75 percent of the greenhouse gases that contribute to global warming. And it's getting worse because we're still not satisfied. Social psychologist Paul Wachtel suggests that the environmental problem of our time is not too many people; it's greed . . . always wanting more. Wachtel embraces an "ecology of satisfaction" to curb the voracious appetite that threatens us with ecological disaster. If you are interested in learning more about ecopsychology, I recommend Roszak's *Ecopsychology: Restoring the Earth, Healing the Mind.* The University of California-Hayward is home to the Ecopsychology Institute and has an Internet website.

*Voluntary simplicity* has to do with living lightly so we can live more fully, and the concept is closely related to ecopsychology. In the sixties and seventies, voluntary simplicity came to be seen as a path away from environmental destruction and toward personal responsibility. It is a practice and for many of us, a purposeful way of living in a fast-paced consumer society. Its philosophy is that we can improve our quality of life and at the same time reduce expenses and environmental impact. The practice is to consciously simplify by gradually releasing those things that consume our daily lives without offering anything in return, thereby reducing our individual and collective environmental impact. It means to ultimately be free from compulsions and attachments, and from the need to possess or control. Simplicity is not poverty. It is a way of life that can elevate the human spirit. A simpler life is a creative balance between poverty and excess. Instead of material riches, voluntary simplicity seeks the invisible wealth of deep purpose, caring, and meaning. At the point that we know we have just enough, not too much and not too little, there is freedom. *Simplicity* by Mark Burch is a manual for personal change that focuses on the benefits of voluntary simplicity and offers exercises for expanding your awareness.

The absence of the feminine in our culture has resulted in the abuse of Mother Earth, just as the extreme patriarchal cultures result in abuse of women and children. **Ecofeminism** is a cutting edge social movement that embraces peace and ecological concerns, while also drawing from ancient sacred traditions. It is a union of both feminism and ecology that embraces issues of race, poverty, sexual preference, child abuse, war, Third World issues, religion, endangered cultures and species, and the global environment. Ecofeminism incorporates womenist values in relation to the natural world, especially the real potential for technology to become a form of suppression and alienation of the human spirit. It values diversity through relationship, the interdependent web of life, and rejection of either/or approaches that encourage exclusion. You can explore these ideas further in *Ecofeminism and the Sacred* by Rosemary Ruether.

## EARTH-BASED RELIGIONS

Earth-based spirituality appeals to those who feel a strong affinity for the earth, for diversity, and for protecting the environment. The three contemporary movements discussed above—ecopsychology, ecofeminism and voluntary simplicity—are the social expressions of earth-centered religions. Women are drawn to earth-centered and Goddess spirituality because they have been left out of mainstream religions where a feminine deity is prohibited. For these women the Goddess fills an empty space in their spiritual quest.

*Paganism* is an umbrella term for the pre-Christian religions that honor many gods and goddesses and have a reverence for all of nature. Women who are drawn to the more mystical path find the pre-Christian belief systems to be much more accommodating of their feminine values and gifts. These ancient religions see nothing unnatural about women using their natural gifts. In paganism a woman can find, among other things, the freedom to make her own decisions about what is best for her. Ritual is a common form of worship that helps to end alienation from the self and the planet, thereby connecting us with our wholeness. Contemporary forms of paganism that are flourishing include Wicca and Native American spirituality.

*Wicca* is a pagan path comprised of a number of traditions that have been created over the years, each with its own set of beliefs, rituals and ethical standards. It appeals to women for the same reasons that other earth-centered religions do. Basic to Wicca is the doctrine, "do as you will, harm no one." As with all earth-based religions, ritual is central to Wicca as a form of self-expression that is healing for women because it helps to break the long history of oppression perpetrated by the patriarchal religions in power today.

**Native American spirituality** was suppressed by the U.S. and Canadian governments for many years. Spiritual leaders were often imprisoned for simply practicing their native rituals. This changed in 1978 when the Freedom of Religion Act was passed. Followers of Native American spirituality usually do not regard their ancient spiritual beliefs as a "religion," in the way that many Christians do. Rather, it is a personal faith that combines Native and Christian elements, along with a trend to return to traditional Native beliefs. The circle is a sacred Native archetype representing wholeness, the fusion of the human and the divine. Integral to Native American spirituality is the belief that no matter who or where we are, we all live on Mother Earth. The ancient Anasazi culture was a Great Mother society. Native American spirituality honors all earthly life, the elders, the ancestors, and the connectedness of all living things. This is why it appeals to so many contemporary women who have felt cut off from their deepest values.

## RE-EMERGENCE OF MARY

Some believe that the Virgin Mary of the Catholic Church is the patriarchy's substitute for the Goddesses of ancient earth-centered religions. For many women the Virgin Mary is not a viable feminine model. She is important only because she gave birth to Jesus and somehow remained a virgin. Christian women are seeking a female spiritual model that is neither virgin nor harlot, but a more realistic Divine Feminine. There is a scholarly resurgence of interest in Mary Magdalene as the personification of a full, vibrant woman, a model of feminine strength and wisdom too long disregarded in mainstream Western religions. Sibohan Houston is a Harvard-educated religious scholar and author of *Invoking Mary Magdalene: Accessing the Wisdom of the Divine Feminine*. According to Houston, Mary Magdalene is mentioned more than any other woman in the New Testament, often spoken of as a wealthy, independent woman who gave Jesus financial support in the early days of his ministry. She had a prominent place in the early Church, yet she was portrayed as a sinful woman. It was Pope Gregory who in the year 591 A.D. pronounced Magdalene a prostitute, and it wasn't until 1969 that the Church rescinded Gregory's declaration. But the tarnished image has remained to affect all women.

Not many people know that the Bible reflects only the Gospels that were chosen by an all-male council. In the 1940s, the Gnostic Gospels were unearthed. These long lost Gospels reflect an equality of male and female, but were excluded from the original Bible. Many who have read Dan Brown's contemporary novel *The Da Vinci Code* are either offended or intrigued by the questions it raises about Christianity, and particularly Brown's claim that the legendary Holy Grail is symbolic of the lost Goddess. It is controversial because it offers a new twist on the story of Jesus and challenges the patriarchy by elevating the feminine. The novel speaks deeply to our longing for the feminine in all areas of our lives.

## WOMEN IN BUDDHISM

At a time in our lives when many of the old forms and institutions are disintegrating and new forms of spirituality are emerging, we more readily have access to the world's ancient spiritual teachings. These ageless wisdom teachings on consciousness are a tremendously rich resource for the Western world and they have brought women into the forefront of Buddhism in America. There have always been great women teachers, but never before have women played the prominent role they do now in Western

Buddhism. In fact, there may be no other main-stream religion in which American women play such an important role. Women such as Pema Chodron, Sharon Salzberg, Ruth Denison, Christina Feldman, and many others, are changing the face of Buddhism as it becomes westernized. They are teaching that emotions are empowering. They are open to the needs of families and a family model of spiritual practice. They are bringing the feminine spiritual values of inclusion and connection to the ancient wisdom teachings and to contemporary religion.

## CONSCIOUS AGING MOVEMENT

As we women reclaim our feminine values and spirituality, our influence is being seen on many fronts. A recent phenomenon is the conscious aging movement that embodies the concepts of later life mental wellness and the spiritual dimensions of aging. It is a movement that affirms the importance of the elder years. The conscious aging paradigm focuses on wisdom and strength instead of loss. Compared to other cultures, we in the U.S. do not value our elders. Until recently, women over fifty have been the most ignored and neglected segment of our population. Typically, the post-childbearing woman becomes invisible to society, and frequently to herself.

As more baby boomers look into the mirror and see their own aging, what can they do with this new awareness? They can get a tummy tuck or a face lift, find new and younger partners, or try other temporary fixes. To age consciously means to acknowledge your value in this life, to see your gifts with new eyes, and to contribute your wisdom to changing the social and personal experience of aging. The energy generated by those who recognize their own worth and value is essential for positively affecting our communities, our world, and future generations. Two special paths that exemplify the conscious aging movement are the return of the Crone and Spiritual Eldering.

The Crone ∞ The word *crone* wasn't always a derogatory term. In pre-Christian times older women were appreciated members of their community. They were leaders, artists, midwives, counselors and healers who were valued as the fulfillment of female life experience and wisdom. Their wisdom grew from a lifetime of commitment, caring, listening, connecting—those values that have always sustained human life. Women of indigenous cultures were not considered wise until post-menopause. Today, thanks to women's efforts to reclaim the feminine, women of midlife and beyond are discovering the strength that comes from knowing who they are. They are freeing themselves of oppressive cultural expectations, accepting themselves just as they are. Choosing the title of Crone is a deliberate act often marked by an initiation ceremony whereby women honor each other with the crown of wisdom. By embracing the title of Crone and valuing their age, women are restoring the image of the Wise Woman to her rightful place of honor and respect.

What is it that calls women from every part of North American to gather at the annual Crones Counsel? What need is met? The Crones Counsel is a call to authenticity, an annual gathering where women can reaffirm their value as women and experience the inspiration of sisterhood. It is common to find three generations of women from the same family attending together. The first Crones Counsel met in 1993 in Jackson Hole, Wyoming. The idea was to have a gathering with no stars, no keynoters, and no hierarchy of organization. It continues to be a yearly celebration where a woman can share her-story and counsel with other women in an environment that promotes equality, encourages diversity, and supports personal empowerment. There is ritual, entertainment, support, and wisdom sharing. Women are encouraged to ask for what they need and want, including a standing ovation as part of their empowering process. It was during my very first Crones Counsel in 1999 that the inspiration for this book was born and was contributed to by several of the wonderful women I met. A natural outgrowth of the Crones Counsel has been the proliferation of regional Crone Circles as a way to regularly connect spiritually with other women. In a society that over-values youth, beauty, sex, speed, and materialism, the Crone movement is a healthy way to foster conscious aging. You can learn more at www.cronescounsel.org.

*Spiritual eldering* is a term coined by Rabbi Zalman Schachter-Shalomi for the potential and process that is open to adults as we age. Reb Zalman founded the Spiritual Eldering Institute in Boulder, Colorado, and is co-author of *From Aging to Sage-ing: A Profound New Vision of Growing Older.* The Spiritual Eldering Institute is a multi-faith organization dedicated to the spiritual dimensions of aging and conscious living. It provides educational programs, trains leaders and professionals to share this work, helps communities and organizations to develop Sage-ing Centers, and builds collaborative relationships in order to share its mission. If we have the potential to live beyond our mid-eighties, it makes sense to live our lives more consciously, connected to supportive community and nature, contributing our values and wisdom to the world and future generations. The conscious aging movement affirms there is a new level of growth awaiting us at midlife and beyond.

The exclusion of women's spirituality has been harmful to women and men alike. Fortunately, many women are reclaiming the ancient forms of spirituality. We now have access to the perennial wisdom of

Eastern religions. The destruction of our environment in the name of profit has spawned movements motivated by a deep concern for life, such as ecopsychology, ecofeminism, voluntary simplicity, and an earth-centered spirituality that appeals to our feminine values. There is a new respect for the wisdom of our elders that is being carried forward by the spiritual eldering and crone movements.

At midlife a woman's spiritual quest includes finding wholeness. Wholeness means integrating the disowned aspects of ourselves so we can grow into our true nature, our souls can express themselves freely, and we can reclaim our original feminine gifts. It takes courage to reach into our depths and retrieve the authentic self. We are challenged to stop, look and listen, to be still and open. The following chapters offer contemporary tools for this inner journey.

EIGHT

# Tools for the Descent

*Standing still,*
*whether in terror or awareness,*
*can be the most moving thing you do.*

—Kati Pressman

Our culture encourages us to live on the surface of our lives—doing, thinking, and identifying with externals. We may not take the time to touch the deeper dimensions of our authentic being until some suffering causes our daily structures and defenses to break down. "Stop, look and listen" isn't just a warning sign for railroad crossings. Stop, look and listen are three personal spiritual tools that will open you to your authentic self. They are perennial wisdom tools for connecting with the silence within and opening yourself to increased awareness. Awareness includes the ability to consciously stand back from your normal reactive patterns and simply be present with what is. Through stillness we can grow in awareness. And because true stillness is so difficult to achieve, this chapter will focus on steps that will help you discover a practice of being still.

## STANDING STILL

There is a vast difference between stillness and being stuck. Stillness is one of the foundations for true wisdom. It is a kind of stopping that allows contacting the wholeness that is within you. On the other hand, stuckness is usually a consequence of fear, self-judgment and busyness. Because the groundlessness of change, loss, and transition is uncomfortable and scary for most of us, it's easy to become frantic to fill the emptiness with busyness. The power in stillness is that it calms the mind and body, allows us to open to what is, and to learn a lot about the workings of our egos. In the moment of connecting with the silence around you, you are not thinking. You are aware, but the inner noise of the mind is still. When you stand still in silence you "see" with new eyes and ears, and this can shift understandings and perceptions of old realities, which then leads to increased awareness. The contemporary spiritual teacher Eckhart Tolle, tells us that stillness is where true wisdom, creativity, and solutions to problems are found. In *Stillness Speaks*, Tolle says, "Wisdom comes with the ability to be still. Just look and just listen. No more is needed. Being still, looking, and listening activates the non-conceptual intelligence within you. Let stillness direct your words and actions." To be still means knowing how to stop.

STOPPING ∽ Stopping is not just slowing down. It is a primer for the more challenging spiritual journey that awaits you. Stopping means doing nothing for a period of time, for the purpose of finding stillness, becoming more aware, and realizing the truth of your authentic self. By stopping, you give yourself the essential gifts of stillness, solitude, and silence. It is a time-out that gives you the freedom to recognize and reorganize your deepest values so that you can live more fully. Stopping is a way to cope with the busyness of your life, a way to hear difficult truths and feelings, a way to wake up to your true self. David Kundtz, author of *Stopping: How to be Still When You Have to Keep Going*, suggests that all you need to do is put space and time around yourself and the mind and soul will sort it out. Your busy self is not your authentic self. Authenticity lies somewhere in between, in the stopping places that are available to you. Stopping is a contemplative practice. It is a tool for coping with the busyness of life that keeps you distracted and unfocused. It allows more receptivity, remembering, and realization.

Kundtz describes three ways of stopping. The first he calls *stillpoints*, the spiritual art of learning to be still in the midst of activity. This means taking advantage of unfilled minutes in your life to do nothing but be fully present with your self in the stillness of the moment. Stillpoints can be found while waiting for a traffic light to change, riding the bus, or watering your plants.

*Stopovers* are mini-vacations for the soul. Whether for an hour or several days, an afternoon or a weekend away, or a structured retreat, stopovers give you the opportunity to purposefully take time out to see what's there in the stillness.

A third kind of stopping is the *grinding halt*. This is usually a significant life transition, one of life's watersheds. A grinding halt often involves a conscious decision to leap into the unknown and be willing to sink or swim for the purpose of working through a life transition.

My first grinding halt came less than three years after my child died. A sense of meaninglessness had been nibbling at me in my quiet moments and it sounded something like this: *It makes no sense to go to work every day, to earn money to pay rent for an apartment I am seldom in, and pay a sitter to care for my child whom I see only nights and weekends.* One golden New England autumn afternoon I was sitting with my mother in her backyard. Out of nowhere I blurted out, "I am going to take a cross-country camping trip." But I had never been out of New England, much less camping. With a growing awareness of my need for something more, I was called to expand my circle of possibilities. In the intervening nine months, I read books on camping, scoured garage sales for used equipment, gathered road maps to guide me, and secured a leave from my dead-end job. The day after my son completed kindergarten we headed west on what was to be a three-month cross-country camping trip. I possessed six hundred dollars, a sturdy old car refurbished by my Dad, and a burning desire to live more fully. And I was fearless. Our three-month camping trip extended into a two-year long odyssey. I never returned to my former life.

When we are ready to move into the next stage of transformation, we are often drawn, consciously or unconsciously, to environments that nurture and support our awakening. These environments can be either spiritual or non-spiritual, psychologically oriented or not. The essential ingredient is that the environment offers safety, freedom, challenge, and authentic relationships. When we find it we know that it is just right for our needs—even though friends and family may think it (and us) strange. In

*Yoga and the Quest for True Self*, Stephen Cope describes the qualities of these transformational spaces. These refuges are temporary safe havens, places for the authentic self to find safety and acceptance. They offer safety through constancy in relationship, such as with a teacher or mentor. It is important that these teachers not be glorified or idolized and that we know they are external representatives of our own true nature. These transformational environments ideally offer an emotional safety that allows trying new ways of being, and recombining, reorganizing, and working through disowned aspects of the self. They provide us with a safe way to find out who we are because they are open to and support our personal development. They are concerned with truth, not doctrine or dogma. They do not exploit vulnerabilities or our shadow side. They do not have to be perfect. What is most important is that we maintain an equal measure of common sense, skepticism and openness. When it's time to move on, we will know.

My second grinding halt came fourteen years later. My son was grown and mostly on his own. One summer day I was watering the front lawn of my home in Boulder, Colorado, when I had an epiphany: *Why am I standing here watering this grass, then fertilizing it to make it grow, so I can mow it endlessly, and pay the never-ending water bills?* It all seemed so meaningless as to make me question the very purpose of my existence. I knew I was ready to risk everything to transcend what I felt was a meaningless life. Shortly thereafter, I manifested an opportunity to live, study and work for a few years at the famed Esalen Institute on the coast of Big Sur, California. For me, as for many spiritual pilgrims from around the world, Esalen has been a truly transformational space. My intuition told me the fit was right, though I couldn't explain why. During three years living and working at Esalen I found the freedom to dance, play and learn, to listen to what was calling me, to live in community, and to heal myself in the stupendous beauty, simplicity and solitude of the land where the mountains meet the ocean. I learned to say good-bye, to let go with ease and gratitude as so many people touched my life and moved on to whatever was calling them. I was exposed to cutting-edge teachers and researchers in the human potential field who planted the seeds for my pursuit of a career in clinical psychology.

However you do it—a stillpoint, stopover, or grinding halt—stopping can be a spiritual tool for finding the stillness to discover your deepest values and meanings. Elsie described her home-leaving journey as one of stopping. She said, "Finally, at midlife my body said 'stop.' I'd exhausted my adrenal system from a lifetime of worrying about what I should be getting done. In leaving home I've given myself the gift of stopping in order to get what I've always wanted: to know myself as God. Even though I'd spent several years as a Catholic nun, I never knew how to do that. Now it means experiencing all things as a seamless whole. We're not a piece of God, we're each wholly God. I get hits of this, but I yearn to fully experience a oneness with all that is."

Every deep yearning is a wish for integration and wholeness. Stopping helps us recognize this yearning, name it, and follow it. As humans we need to stop in order to notice what our body might be telling us. Learn to listen to your body. If you pay attention to body messages, it will tell you when you are in balance or if something in your life needs to change. Listen to your patterns of illness: What is that headache or backache telling you? Are you tired all the time? If so, try to identify what might be draining your energy. Do you frequently catch colds? Perhaps your immune system is depleted because you don't respect your need for rest. Don't wait until, like Elsie, your whole system breaks down before giving yourself the gift of stopping.

LOOKING ∾ Each of the senses is a miracle. We do not realize how little we actually hear, see, smell, taste or feel as we go about our daily lives. For years we can walk down the same avenue or drive through the same neighborhood and never quite see it, although the eyes are taking it in. We do a lot of looking without really noticing, without paying attention. True attention is considered a profound spiritual response because it deepens awareness. When you are aware you notice at increasingly deeper levels. Looking deeply, paying attention to your inner and outer landscape, will help you to grow in awareness. At first, the physical senses may predominate. You may simply notice the air moving in and out as you breathe, your chest rising and falling, the room temperature on your skin. Looking more deeply opens awareness of the thoughts marching across your mind. You may notice thoughts speeding by and distracting you, or perhaps they float away like bubbles. The trick to being more aware is simply to notice what's there without reacting. When you do, you are cultivating the priceless gift of insight. Looking still deeper opens awareness to feelings lying just beneath the surface. More than anything, attention is an act of connection. It can reveal the subtle interface between feelings and thoughts. There may be anger, loneliness, unresolved grief, a sense of peace, or expansive joy. Being aware of your inner life connects you to your true self. The reward is always authenticity.

LISTENING ✍ An integral part of looking deeply is listening. Deep listening is another way of using the senses to pay attention, a way in which the small inner voice can be heard. Because deep listening requires total concentration, it is challenging work. When we really listen, we notice our feelings and thoughts, how we relate to our body, the way we interact with others. Our un-listened-to feelings wreak havoc with the mind and the body. Emotional pain turned against the self contributes to a range of physical and emotional problems. Have you ever walked into a room where people were in conversation, and had an unfamiliar reaction triggered in you? For some reason the scene activates an out-of-awareness emotion, possibly a repressed wish to be seen or included, or a wish to run away out of fear or shyness. That emotional response blinds you to what is actually happening. Un-listened-to feelings also contribute to violence, depression, alienation from self and others, and a host of psychosomatic illnesses.

Modern neuroscience research reveals that we humans do not stop developing until we die, that we are continually forming new brain neurons on the basis of our daily experience, and that we can profoundly shape our relation to experience by paying attention to it. The more we pay attention by using our senses, the more we influence the brain and body at the cellular level. It is easy to be out of touch with the senses. I urge you to develop an appreciation for your amazing sensing abilities, for they are the messengers of your soul. If you cannot listen deeply to yourself, how can you listen to another?

When I asked Elsie what was calling her to leave home, she replied, "My heart told me to sell my house and get rid of all my belongings. I'd been looking at how one lives from the heart instead of head. I didn't know anything about that, though most people saw me as a heartful and helpful caregiver. I despaired when I examined what it meant to listen to my heart. How would I know? Such a mystery to me. The rational, logical mind had always ruled my life. So I've been learning to listen to my heart because right now my life depends on it."

Standing still—stopping, looking, listening—enables you to recognize the truth of your experience. If you can't see what is true, how can you recognize what's not true? Listening to your heart, to the quiet inner voice, is not simple. It takes time for the mind chatter to quiet down. In the silence of stillness you will begin to know what you feel, you will open to what is calling you, to your truth. You may experience silence as a dreaded loneliness and isolation. The main difference between solitude and loneliness is an intimacy with your self. What is your capacity for aloneness? The inner work here is to recognize the spiritual obstacle of fear of aloneness. If you recognize this tendency in yourself, I suggest you reread chapter 5. Stillness and solitude are necessary for the soul. Practicing stillness will move you to the higher consciousness that is the fruit of the spiritual journey. Be still and listen.

*I want to know if you can be alone*
*with yourself*
*and if you truly like the company you keep*
*in the empty moments.*

—Oriah Mountain Dreamer

## EXERCISE

Think back to a time or place when you enjoyed the tranquility of solitude. Where were you? What did it feel like? Make a list of three ways that can bring more of these moments into your life. Once you've identified a few different ways, make a date with yourself and schedule a weekly solitude break in your calendar. Following are some ideas to get you started.

❖ Inspirational reading or music

❖ Journal writing

❖ Visual beauty such as flowers, art, color

❖ Being in nature or with animals

❖ Meditation, prayer, sacred rituals

❖ A regular silent retreat at monastery

## STANDING OPEN

In the previous section you saw that standing still is a way to listen to your life, to hear what there is to hear. Listening is more effective with openness. Openness is the ability to receive whatever the world offers and to learn the lessons of life because you've noticed them. When you notice and learn, there is a feedback loop of information and growth: you are open, you notice, you learn. Most of us spend much of our life asleep. It usually takes a wake up call of some consequence, such as a loss or major life change, to shake us awake enough to see with new eyes, to hear with new ears.

Initiations educate the soul. By midlife you, like most women, have been through several initiations: graduations, marriages, childbirth, loss of parents or other loved ones, loss of health or career. All were stepping stones that initiated you out of innocence and pushed the boundaries of your life toward transition. A painful initiation for many of the women I interviewed was loss of the mother role. Jana said, "I had no clue as to the meaning of my existence once my mother role ended. It was a big wake-up call, a sense of urgency to discover my purpose and meaning. I had to look anew at whether I was going to live or die." The soul of a woman is developed within the context of the familiar ties that she carries with her always. As old roles and identities slip away, what looms is the inevitable descent into the unknown.

Any descent into the unknown begins with the loss of innocence, a need to die to the familiar . . .

some form of leaving behind to follow what is calling you. What then is required of you? It helps to decide to surrender to a guidance that is deeper than your small, personality self. Phyllis described her experience quite poignantly: "I had to open to see things that were being given to me that I had been blind to. It took all being ripped away to arrive at this place. I had to give up, let go, ask for guidance from several sources: from my soul when it finally opened so I could hear it's voice, or the universal energy that surrounds me, or grace, God, Holy Spirit—it's all the same to me."

A true descent breaks the old ways of being and refines us so we feel more deeply and recognize what has value and meaning. A descent into the darkness destroys the habitual patterns by which we've established our security. Genuine descent asks us to be willing to not know where we are going, to not know what is next, to strike out on our own, alone, and face our shadow side. Going into this abyss can be very frightening and requires a warrior-like energy, as well as being open to all situations, feelings and people. As awareness grows, we are more able to work with the difficult emotions of shame, fear, and self-judgment, and to be open to whatever is there—to be present.

Spiritual maturity is the ability to live with ambiguity and uncertainty. When women leave home, a common mistake is to go right into another relationship, a natural urge to *do* something rather than stay in the uncomfortable emptiness of the unknown. To resist this urge requires trust and self-compassion. We cannot be open if we are awash in self-criticism and are afraid of our shadow side. It may be helpful at this point to review the section on self-compassion in chapter 5. We live in a culture that values the idea of a prearranged life plan and the use of will to hammer the self into an ideal shape. The mind is supposed to identify goals and then the will is supposed to force us into that shape. This is an externally imposed, mechanical approach that does not work with the rhythm of our own souls. It has nothing to do with accessing our inner wisdom, or listening to our true self.

A daily twenty-minute practice of any method of stillness can move you through the normal fear of the emptiness that is part of any transformation. As you begin to practice stillness you may become aware of your inner critic, possibly old parental messages that criticize taking time for yourself, the gremlin voice that says, "do something productive." This distracting inner chatter wants to cover up fear. Just follow the disturbance, being present to it without judgment . . . simply being open. Eventually the chatter calms down. When you become more comfortable with being still and open, try to name the fear, or journal about it, or to talk to a supportive friend. In one of his workshop at Estes Park, Colorado, Thich Nhat Hanh said, "The present moment is where life can be found, and if you don't arrive there, you miss your appointment with life." To help us arrive in the present, he teaches the powerful practice of breathing in and saying, 'I have arrived' and then breathing out saying, 'I am home.'

The remainder of this chapter offers several time-honored spiritual tools for cultivating stillness, openness and awareness. They are practical techniques derived from the ancient wisdom traditions. Most are grounded in finding stillness and openness through some form of meditative practice that helps you to notice and allow feelings, bodily sensations, or thoughts, and to put space around your normal reactive patterns. When everything is equally allowed to come into awareness, the mind and the heart are open. This is all you need to do. This in itself is a spiritual practice.

## MINDFULNESS

Mindfulness is simply a way of being connected to the silence within. It is a way to notice, to pay attention to your inner rhythm. There are many forms of mindfulness practice, and you may have heard of or practiced one or more of them. Most are rooted in the ancient Eastern philosophies that offer

wisdom for living more peacefully and compassionately, for being more awake, and for causing no harm
to self or others. We frequently cause harm by grasping at experiences and hanging onto things that are
impermanent. By not grasping, by practicing letting
go, we can bring awareness to that part of ourselves
that never feels satisfied. Then we have choice. This
philosophy of mindfulness is the bedrock of Eastern
spiritual wisdom.

Of all the meditation practices that have been
taught, mindfulness is one of the most profound. It is
the oldest form of meditation and is also the simplest, being least bound by formal ritual. Mindfulness
refers to practices for the mind that develop calm
through sustained attention, and insight through
reflecting and noticing what is. It is often referred to
as the medicine that cures the disease of desire.
Instead of feeling deficient or deprived, the practice
of mindfulness brings a feeling of nourishment and
abundance. A fundamental technique for paying
attention is focusing awareness on the body while
sitting or walking. Reflection occurs quite naturally
as you become comfortable with meditating, as you
look inward and become acquainted with how your
mind works. This constant and sustained investiga-
tion called mindfulness is the primary focus of
Insight Meditation. When coupled with compassion,
mindfulness is a powerful and effective way to work

with difficult emotions by developing an observer self. When we are both participant and observer, there can be a spirit of kindness and acceptance toward whatever is there, moment by moment. I appreciate mindfulness meditation because it relates to practitioners as spiritual friends and avoids the authoritarian structure of more formal spiritual practices. The two exercises that follow are adapted from Barbara Fishman.

BREATH AWARENESS ✑ Find a comfortable position sitting or kneeling, using a cushion, bench or chair. Keep your spine straight, but don't force your body into a position it isn't used to. Close your eyes and turn your attention inward. Find the place where breathing feels most obvious to you, generally the abdomen or the nostrils. Bring your attention to that place and try to keep it there without forcing. Simply notice the bare sensations of breathing. Let go of distractions. Your mind will wander, so without judgment let the thoughts go and gently bring your attention back to breathing. Don't try to stop thinking because you can't. Just let go of thought once you recognize it and return awareness to the breath. Be patient and gentle with yourself. Begin with five or ten minutes and aim to build your practice time to forty minutes each day.

BODY AWARENESS ✑ Lie on the floor or a bed with your eyes closed. Turn your full attention to your body. Take some slow, deep breaths down into your belly. Let your body become very heavy. Bring your awareness to the left side of the body and slowly scan for sensations. Do the same for the right side. Then do the same for the whole body. Continue to breathe gently and stay in touch with the surface you are lying on. Notice the stillness. Are there areas in your body that feel calm, open, pleasant? Then slowly open your eyes and sit quietly, maintaining the stillness as you bring yourself back into the room. What messages does your body have for you? If you pay attention to body messages, you'll know when things are okay or are not the way you want them to be. As you rise and go about your day, remember the stillness and know you can always return to it.

In each moment and during any activity, you have a chance to wake up by being more aware of your bodily sensations. Watch what your mind is doing. The practice is to ask your self, "What's happening now?" in order to increase mindfulness. Then ask, "How am I relating to this?" in order to see whether you are reacting or simply observing. If you experience a reaction, can you let it go? The Buddha said that freedom through mindfulness comes slowly, like filling a bucket drop by drop. Each moment of clearly seeing what is there and then letting it be, is a significant drop in your bucket. One day the bucket overflows.

## YOGA

When in my mid-twenties, I injured my lower back trying to play tennis. The pain running down my left leg was so intense I could barely drag my leg, and the deep tendon reflexes of my knee and heel were numbed. I went to an orthopedist who spoke of back surgery. About that same time I stumbled upon a magazine article about the benefits of yoga and it spoke deeply to me. I soon found a local yoga class and told the teacher about my pain. It was almost too painful to lower myself onto the yoga mat that first day. The teacher generously said to me, "If you do everything I say and stop when I tell you, I guarantee you will be well in six weeks." Well, I was completely pain free in three weeks. When I returned to the orthopedist and told him my experience, he said, "You don't think I can prescribe yoga to my patients, do you?" I have practiced yoga in one form or another to this day.

Millions of Americans now practice some form of yoga on a regular basis—in health clubs, senior centers, retreat centers, and on their living room floors. Hatha yoga emphasizes specific yoga postures in combination with controlled breathing. Sports teams, Hollywood stars, and mainstream television programming have adopted it. The physical benefits of yoga are well documented by medical research. These benefits include improved cardiovascular health, weight loss, and improved strength and flexibility. Yoga tunes the body's organ systems; it brings relaxation and reduces stress so we breathe and sleep better; it cultivates calmness to help control reactivity and unhealthy desires; it develops focus and discipline. Yet many people are not aware that yoga is a four thousand-year-old practical spiritual path that can bring a renewed sense of purpose and a more satisfying life, and it does not require leaving our everyday life. Yoga has its own ancient spiritual philosophy and psychology of practice, with lots of complicated, esoteric theory that the interested seeker can pursue, if desired.

After leaving Esalen, I was called to experience a spiritual community. This led me to visit the Kripalu Center for Yoga and Health in Lenox, Massachusetts. Kripalu, an intentional community founded in the early seventies by Amrit Desai, is based on a Hindu religious philosophy and is named for Desai's own teacher, Swami Shri Kripalvanandji. Kripalu grew from a small ashram in rural Pennsylvania to become the largest residential yoga community in the United States. It occupies a four-story brick building on lovely grounds purchased from the Jesuits, and houses hundreds of residents and guests from around the world who come to workshops, retreats, and to learn health and healing practices. I entered Kripalu's Spiritual Life Training program and lived for six months in its intense spiritual environment. Here I was immersed in an authentic semi-monastic lifestyle of yoga and meditation, macrobiotic diet, *seva* (selfless work), and nightly *satsang* (chanting). Each day began at 4:30 am and ended by 9 pm.

Sometimes we need a stopping place, a transformational space to support us on the journey to true self. Both Esalen and Kripalu were transformational places for me. My experience of Kripalu was one of being wrapped in a soft, warm blanket, while Esalen allowed my long-neglected wild child to come out and play and introduced me to the many faces of the human potential. While different in many aspects, both Esalen and Kripalu are on the circuit for modern day spiritual pilgrims seeking integration of body, mind and spirit, or simply a refuge from the rapid pace of modern life.

One of the benefits of yoga to the Western seeker is that it teaches about presence. This is accomplished by using the breath and body postures to increase energy and awareness. Body postures called *asanas* draw the senses inward and improve emotional balance, energize the body, and allow connection with our true nature. The inner mental focus is useful for people who are vulnerable to fear or are easily overwhelmed by emotions. The gift of yoga is learning to be present with your own experience, whether emotional or physical, as the life force is grounded through physical movements and conscious breathing. The body is active while the mind observes the breath. The breath is a conduit for integrating the emotional and physical bodies, and has the potential to open areas that have been frozen or exiled. As more awareness is brought to these dormant places, the energy flows and you begin to open. Similar to mindfulness meditation, the practice is to be present with your inner experience. You breathe, relax, feel, and allow.

Yoga is meditation in motion. You do not have to study Buddhism to meditate, nor do you need to study yoga's esoteric foundations to benefit. Increasing awareness of your body and its needs creates balance in your life. There is the satisfaction of nurturing and caring for you. Through hatha yoga, you are more likely to know when to stop and rest, when you are hungry or full, and what you feel.

## INTUITION

When was the last time you found yourself thinking, "If only I'd listened to my intuition," or how often have you had an experience and then said, "I should have known better than to ignore my intuition"? Intuition is the subtle voice of your true self. It is a form of higher guidance. Do you neglect your intuition because you are too busy, or because you have been trained to look outside of yourself for answers? In a similar vein, how can you know that information you gather from outside of yourself will benefit you? Intuition is the act of inner knowing or sensing that bypasses the mind's rational thinking. It is a direct knowing that is not yet evident or proven. Only by listening to, respecting, and fine-tuning your intuition can you truly know if something is right for you.

I asked Sophia if trust was validated for her when she listened to her intuition. "Following my intuition challenges all my beliefs about security. I have learned that I have a limited view of what is possible. When I am willing to let go and open to possibilities, they show up better than I'd dreamed. That makes life interesting. It invites surrender. I like to think that the universe has a larger vision for us than we have for ourselves. As a guiding principle it seems to be true. I'm not sure how much is the grand design and how much we ourselves embody and are the conduits of its expression. I do see I'm part of a greater whole where there's a larger design at work.

"I frequently feel frustrated because I don't see the big picture or have a clear sense of my purpose as I'd like. It's challenging to trust my intuition in relationship to the Divine. Here I'm treading on theology. My question right now is, when a door doesn't open, how much is my responsibility to push on it— rather than relaxing into the idea that it wasn't meant to be, that God has something better in mind, or it's not my destiny. Mastering my issues of security and surrender is a life process I continue to stumble my way through."

Security issues imply change and the love-hate relationship we all have with change. We want spiritual growth, yet fear it because we know that change often means loss of one thing in order to have another. Given that we are all human beings living in physical bodies, wanting self-understanding and to live more consciously, we are still subject to the way the mind filters our perceptions. Information is first filtered through our needs, beliefs and life experiences, and something always gets lost in the translation. In this way, intuition can be distorted.

What is the difference between internal and external forms of guidance? Is one "higher" than another? I believe both are important. At the beginning of the spiritual journey you may find that external guidance is primarily available to you in the form of a teacher, twelve-step program, a guru, or a group of like-minded seekers. People often go to spiritual retreats and self-help workshops for external guidance. However, relying solely on external sources of guidance can become another addiction used to avoid you. But as you begin to develop mindfulness, to be still and more open to what is, to notice and pay attention, you will find that you can trust your intuition. This inner guidance is the fruit of your spiritual practice.

## LABYRINTH

The labyrinth is a walking meditation that has been rediscovered as the contemplative tool that it is. Rev. Lauren Artress of Grace Cathedral in San Francisco is credited with reclaiming the labyrinth as a form of modern day pilgrimage. In *Walking a Sacred Path: Rediscovering the Labyrinth as a Spiritual Tool*, Artress says, "Grace Cathedral is determined to be a leader in reclaiming the walking meditation as part of the Christian tradition, and to be a source to guide others in the use of the labyrinth as a spiritual tool."

In 1999 Artress started The Labyrinth Network in order to establish communities of people who gather to use the labyrinth as a tool for meditation, prayer, group ritual, and transformation. She envisions it as a spiritual network for addressing social issues such as violence, extended families, victims of violence, people facing life-threatening diseases, or rite-of-passage rituals for adolescents. People are attracted to the labyrinth because of its potential as a healing tool. It is possible to deepen self-awareness, empower creativity, focus the mind, and gain insight into the spiritual journey.

When Rebecca left home after heeding the wake-up call of uterine cancer, she was intuitively drawn to the healing powers of the labyrinth. She trained with Dr. Artress at Grace Cathedral and now offers the labyrinth to others. Rebecca speaks of the labyrinth as a metaphor for personal transformation and tells us why it has returned today as a spiritual tool.

The labyrinth is an ancient mystical tool that can bring about a shift in consciousness. It is meant to awaken us to the deep rhythm that unites us to ourselves and to the light within. For centuries people of many traditions have walked the labyrinth to deepen their connection to the quiet. It is possible to find the earliest forms of labyrinths in the Ukraine, where they date back to around 8,000 BC. Ancient labyrinths have also been found in Peru's Inca culture, in India, Iceland, Scandinavia, the British Isles, and in North America—specifically Mexico and the Southwestern United States.

They can be found in many religious traditions, in various forms, around the world. One of the oldest and most famous of the medieval labyrinths is inside Chartres Cathedral in Chartres, France. The Jewish Kabbala, the Hopi Medicine Wheel and the Tibetan Sand Mandala are further examples of labyrinths. They are made of many different materials: turf, tile, stone, mosaic, and canvas just to name a few. For young children and others who might not have access to walking labyrinths, finger labyrinths exquisitely carved in wood are available.

Labyrinths are mysterious because we do not know the origin of their design, but it is believed to

have evolved out of the spiral pattern found everywhere in nature. Examples of nature's spirals are
seashells, the pinecone, the simple circle of the sun
and moon. The spiral was the most sacred symbol of
Neolithic Europe. Most labyrinths are circular—large
enough to be walked into emotionally, physically and
spiritually—and have a purposeful path to be walked
from the outer edge to the center and back out
again. It is not a maze or a puzzle intended to confuse
you. Rather, it is a single path and a space that can
increase your capacity for reflection and receptivity.
Once you make the choice to enter the labyrinth,
the path becomes a metaphor for your own journey
through life. There is no wrong or right way to walk
and, as in life, you do so at your own natural pace.
Walking the labyrinth, and all that happens on it, is
grasped through your intuitive, pattern-discerning
faculty. It is open to anyone, from any tradition, does
not require a doctrine or belief system. It can be
walked, danced, or crawled. You cannot fail; the
labyrinth is very user friendly.

As a labyrinth facilitator, Rebecca suggests walking the labyrinth in three stages.

(1) Release: walking into the labyrinth is a time
to release your troubles, quiet your mind and open
your heart to whatever you feel. Become aware of
your breathing. Take slow breaths. Relax and move
at your own pace. (2) Receive: reaching the center of

the circle can be a metaphor for finding home, a place of meditation or prayer. Pause, open to your higher power, and listen to your small inner voice. Feel the safety and have a heart-to-heart talk with yourself. (3) Return: when you are ready, begin walking out by following the same path. As you follow the path out, you might experience the sense of well-being, healing, excitement, or peace, metaphorically reconnecting with the outside world.

In its highest form the labyrinth is a metaphor for the journey through transformation and return to the ordinary. Its relevance today has to do with the return of the feminine principle discussed in chapter 7. In walking the labyrinth people sense that it is feminine in its organic, non-linear, unfolding way; in its ancient wisdom; and in its potential for community and wholeness. There are no splits or divisions between mind, body, psyche or spirit. Walking in this non-linear way opens us to the possibility of seeing our innate wholeness.

The tools reviewed in this chapter have a beautiful common thread that will help you to slow down and open to your inner self. Mindfulness meditation, yoga, intuition, and the labyrinth are everyday tools for finding the stillness within you. They allow you to step outside the busy-ness of life for a moment and enter your inner temple. Through stillness you can open to the scary places within, make wise choices, and find compassion for yourself. Stillness is not a state of ignorance or not knowing. Rather, it is intelligence . . . consciousness without form. We live in a culture that is trying to run away from stillness and into noise, materialism, wanting more of everything. Stillness tools will help you to meet yourself on the midlife woman's spiritual path to authenticity.

*It's important to hear about this in-between state. Otherwise we think the warrior's journey is one way or the other, either we're all caught up or we're free. The fact is that we spend a long time in the middle. This juicy spot is a fruitful place to be. Resting here completely— steadfastly experiencing the clarity of the present moment—is called enlightenment.*

—Pema Chodron

NINE

# *Tools for the Ascent*

*In spiritual work, turning a circle is
closer to the truth than turning a corner.*

—Kati Pressman

Unless you have the ability to live in a cloistered
or monastic setting, it becomes necessary to
work out ways to be in the world while your inner
work is progressing. It is not necessary (or practical)
to come to a total standstill in your physical life
while moving forward with the inner work. Spiritual
work is ongoing with no definable end point, no corner to turn. We never finish growing toward higher
levels of consciousness and deeper awareness. As

seen in the previous chapter, the inner work of spiritual growth asks that you stop, pay attention, and listen more deeply to your inner voice. Learning to stand still and be open to what *is* will help you tolerate the emptiness and anxiety that is part of any life shift. As you become more authentic and attuned to your true nature, you will be more open, more able to accept what is, to speak your truth, let go, grieve your losses, and feel compassion for yourself. This inner work will allow you to bring your authentic self into the world where it belongs, where it is needed today.

After every life shift there is a need for reorientation. Transition has a life of its own and doesn't like you to try to hurry it along. Give yourself the time you need to get used to the inner and outer changes. Accept that transition is a process. Resist the urge to "do something" before knowing what is needed. Premature action is usually fear's response to the unknown. Bring compassion to your fear. Whether you have chosen your life shift or it was chosen for you, you can trust that it is a gift of learning. You can trust that the gifts of your descent, of going deeply into yourself, will not let you down. It is not an easy task finding your way in the outer world while the inner spiritual work goes on. There are certain practical matters worthy of your attention as you recreate a life in the world. You might find that letting go of out-dated roles and attitudes that stifle your creativity is helpful as you approach these matters.

## RE-CREATION MATTERS

The process of re-creation is all about constructing a life in which your authentic self can thrive. The reorientation that brings us back into relation with life cannot be rushed. One foot needs to be firmly grounded in the outer world, while the other foot is planted in the ongoing work of the spirit. Paying attention to both inner and outer life is necessary as the pieces of you begin to reshape themselves. Two essential reminders are: (1) maintain compassion and acceptance toward your self, and (2) be consistently honest about your feelings and perceptions. Here is a quote from my journal sixteen months into my journey.

*Stopping again, finally, for a winter. Somehow I needed to return to my roots, my first neighborhood, to see the house I loved so long ago. I trust that it is the right thing to do. Walking now in the sweet neighborhood park, alongside the old creek, my dog at my side, my beloved Flatirons looming in the pure blue sky—I feel held. I need to be held after years of alienation. I have a new sense of belonging, being in this place, walking these paths. A sense of belonging and solidness is growing in me, as though I've finally touched base, found my ground again. Healing is possible here as I reconnect with the person I was before I lost myself to a relationship years ago. That person is wiser now, more open and full, richer in values, poorer in material possessions. This returning is a balm for my wounds. In this little community I can rebuild home for myself. I feel ready to reach out and connect, to give and receive, to live through feelings of relatedness—to people, nature, society, the universe, and myself.*

The journey to authenticity is about listening to your own guidance, befriending and caring for your true self. Often this means finding your unique way to express your creative self. Natalie Goldberg is a well-known writer who taught me about morning pages—a writing practice anybody can use. Each morning set aside fifteen to thirty minutes to write non-stop by hand. This is a solitary discipline that activates intuitive flow, clears emotional debris, and opens creativity. All the quotes from my Journal shared in this book come from my own morning pages. Yes, it takes time and the ability to be still, as any discipline does. But it will open you to your own creative source. The stories in this book reveal the many ways courageous women have found their creative expression. When Jana was recovering strength lost by her multiple surgeries, part of her physical therapy included breath retraining. She had a life-changing spiritual experience through breath work that opened her to heightened hearing, sight, and clairvoyance. This spontaneous experience led Jana to train as a professional breath work facilitator, and this is how she found her source of creative expression.

One dreary winter day in the midst of my own dark night of the soul, I visited an art museum for respite. My soul longed for something I didn't yet recognize I needed. I was depressed, discouraged, down in the dumps. As I wandered through the art galleries I suddenly noticed my visual and cognitive perceptions sharpening—details and colors were heightened, images appeared to be three dimensional, and the insights triggered by the paintings were integrated spontaneously. Afterwards, I noticed my mind was extraordinarily clear, I was totally present with my environment and myself. Since childhood I have been an artistic soul: drawing, the fiber arts, sewing, painting in different media. But I had abandoned art years ago in favor of more intellectual pursuits. The art museum experience was a poignant reminder that I need creative expression in my life in order to be fully alive. When my creativity is accessed my spirit is lightened.

If you've ignored your need for creative expression, you can be sure it will emerge at midlife. If you do not express your creativity, if you do not listen to your own being, you will have betrayed yourself. Notice and welcome sources of inspiration in your life that reveal what is authentic in you. It helps to free up your creativity by releasing your inner critic's ideas of right and wrong. The thirteenth century Persian poet, Rumi, said that unlimited creativity is always available when we are connected to our authenticity. I am awed by how the women I interviewed found the courage to bring their gifts and talents into the world in ways they or their families could never have imagined. Not only are they giving to the world, but they are nourishing their authentic selves as well.

Diana is an example of a woman reclaiming her creativity at midlife. She mused, "I'd been so shut down, doing what was expected of me as wife, mother, daughter—all those roles. Yet my creativity was emerging. I had an affair, and through my activities with that man I glimpsed another part of myself—an exuberant, creative self I didn't recognize. I made a spiritual choice to invest in my own learning by going to mime school—because I must do work that is fulfilling, creative, and makes my soul sing, because I'm worth it. This required me to trust in the face of fear and disapproval. In choosing to give up my beloved family I gave myself to the greater purpose of living my soul purpose." Today Diana is an artist, storyteller, and a face painter who designs and provides programs for children's parties and schools using mime, story, song and art to teach children self-love and respect for others.

Mari left her young family when such an action was unthinkable. Today, with a doctorate in education, she has a healthy relationship with her three adult children and their families. Over the years Mari has published two books and has made hundreds of presentations worldwide to help build family strengths, foster kids' resilience, prevent violence, and raise self-esteem in children and the adults who care for them. Her creative contribution to the world is to help youngsters become caring, confident, competent, and connected.

Two of the women whose stories contributed to this book were already accomplished artists when their life shift occurred. As a painter, Ann found herself wrestling with *how* she wants her art to be out in the world, rather than just "making it" as an artist. Her journey has been about "truly exploring all the edges through creative expression of *myself*. I have done radical things, expressive things, to see who I am, how I fit into the landscape, find out my real response by pushing up against new things. Today, my growing edge is dealing with the world as it is. I don't want my authentic self to get squelched by marketing my art. My issue is to *know* my real self rather than *prove* my self-worth through my art. I've always sacrificed my authentic self until now."

Voncille's story has a different but equally important twist. Voncille moved into her art studio when she left home, her twin teenagers, and an emotionally needy husband of thirty-three years. "My husband began to get a life once I left. He began to relate more with friends and to paint. He painted voraciously, and by the end of the six months I was gone he had his own one-man show. When we resumed our life together, it was on very different terms."

Ann, Voncille, Mari and Diana tapped into their creative source only after recreating themselves. Today, each woman is giving back to the world in meaningful ways.

## CHOICE MATTERS

Do you believe that you *are* the choices you have made? If so, it will be useful to look at your own pattern of choice-making, the chain of choices that has made up your life to this point. Look at the how, when and what of the choices you have made. Many women are frightened of making choices because choosing one way usually involves relinquishing something else. Such are the ups and downs of choice and compromise. We are terrified of being wrong when we can't blame anyone else. A bad choice is not the same as wrong choice. A bad choice usually comes from self-destructive behaviors rooted in lack of awareness and self-betrayal. We can't know if a choice is wise or wrong until we've lived with it. But we can know that a choice generally results in a change in direction. Scary? Just when you think you are safe and secure, there is a systemic shift of some sort, and new choices are required.

As you embark on the outer aspect of your journey, whether you are starting your life over from scratch or not, take the time to reflect on the choices you've made in the past, as well as on your style of choice making. Are you impulsive, deliberate, or avoidant? Do you make choices from your intellect, your heart, or your intuition? Are your choices based on another person's expectations? Are you comfortable with your style of decision making? Is it driven by fear or by awareness? It has been said that choice is destiny's soul mate. The saddest thing is being trapped in limitations of our own creation. As you explore the matter of your destiny, take into consideration the woman you will be a year from now—hopefully a more knowledgeable and aware woman coping with today's choices.

## ATTITUDE MATTERS

By the time a woman reaches midlife she has met her biological and relational obligations. Perhaps she is more comfortable in her own skin and just wants to accept herself, to claim her feminine gifts, and to speak her truth. Success and prosperity dilemmas present themselves in a new light at midlife and often require a change in attitude. Attitude is a state of mind that reflects your stance toward life—positive, neutral, or negative. When you change your way of looking at things, you change your attitude.

Many women have derived their sense of self from a lifetime of giving to others. At midlife there is a healthy shift toward learning to ask and to receive. There will always be things you can't count on or control: the weather, family, other people's intentions, or a loved one's understanding. The challenge here is to expand your options by asking, "Who and what is there for me?" and to be flexible, open, and present with what is. If you don't give yourself permission, nobody else will give it to you. Openness allows you to notice your resistance to the truth of your needs. You can run or you can stop, look and listen. You can stand still and pay attention to what is. You can also dive down deep to find what is true for you. Diana, speaking of openness and trust, said, "The world is my garden. I accept the moment, do what I have to do, and life flows."

Expanding your circle of trust and support is an important asset on this journey. You may ask yourself, "How do I achieve more trust? How do I know if I am doing it right?" These are normal questions. There may be negative feedback from friends and family. These people have been the frame of reference within which you compared and defined yourself. They provided you with the filter through which you have judged yourself. Conventional psychological wisdom is that when you change a behavior, the new behavior provides direct evidence upon which new beliefs and attitudes can be built. As you expand your radius of trust and support, and as you experiment with small incremental changes, you will have direct experience of the effects on your attitudes and beliefs. You are then free to judge for yourself. "It's your unique journey," said Elsie. "You must do it alone, but you will need the support of others. There is no going back once the journey begins, so it's no good looking back with regret. Jump in and swim, especially when feeling vulnerable, scared, fatigued or lonely."

The attitudes of success and abundance demand examination by any woman who has had a life shift and found herself on this midlife journey without a map. Many women of the baby boomer generation define themselves as successful when they have attained unprecedented career status and financial freedom. They attuned themselves to the mainstream culture of driven-ness and made significant compromises to attain success. At midlife a core shift occurs, whether listened to or not. A woman is called to re-examine her values, relationships, and attitudes. As awareness and wisdom increase with age, she learns that what she really wants is to connect more deeply to herself and relate to others from the heart. She

wants the level of intimacy she has found with girlfriends. Elsie, whose leaving home journey was initiated with a cessation of striving, spoke poignantly of
the meaninglessness of career and material success.
Her deepest longing was to find "oneness with all
that is." Once we connect intimately with ourselves,
there is a natural longing for wholeness, to align
body, mind and spirit. At midlife, true success is
often equated with freedom, generosity, passion,
commitment, and self-expression. The fundamental
question becomes, "Who am I being?" rather than,
"What am I doing?"

Abundance is an attitude, a mind set. Much
depends on your beliefs about the source of abundance. You create your experience of abundance (or
lack thereof) every moment of your life. You are free
to choose an attitude of abundance or scarcity, of
prosperity or lack. I am not speaking of affluence,
though that is one definition of abundance—but of a
deep fullness created by the flow of love, money and
relatedness. By developing your spiritual self you are
aligning with the many channels through which true
success and abundance flow. You attract abundance
by participating in its flow. This means to give of
yourself and to take responsibility for what you do
have. As you circulate your true riches, the circle of
goodness broadens to include you. Take a moment to
examine your attitude toward abundance. Can you

trust you will have abundance if you allow it? Think bigger than you are accustomed to. Reclaim the inspirations and ideas that nourish you, for they will attract true abundance. Focus on what you want instead of what you don't want. Feel gratitude for what you do have and share it with others. Gratitude is an attitude and a choice. The more you are consciously grateful, the more you will attract things and people to be grateful for. Fall in love with the process, not the result.

This book was born by attraction. Even though I couldn't see the road in front of me, I trusted the rightness of the journey and plunged ahead. My passion, beliefs and openness were unbounded. Without looking or asking, the women whose stories guided this book came seemingly out of nowhere and freely shared their wisdom. Every resource I needed came to me without seeking. This phenomenon supports my belief that when we are ready and open, the teacher appears. When we live from true self, abundance flows. I attracted the richness and depth of these stories because I resonate with the integrity of the journey. I continue to marvel at the universal law of attraction.

MONEY MATTERS

Letting go of excess baggage is not a new ideal. Throughout history the world's great teachers—Jesus,

St. Francis, Mother Theresa, Gandhi and Thoreau, among others, advocated a life of few possessions. The back-to-the-land movement of the sixties further advanced the idea of owning less, working less, and needing less so as to focus on what is truly important. This could be spirituality, freedom, social action, or living more authentically. People who found the mainstream culture's definition of success and abundance to be unsatisfactory and disappointing have adopted the philosophy of voluntary simplicity. Being able to live through a major life transition frequently requires decreasing the pressure to earn money and manage material possessions in order to keep life's precious options open. Whether we call it voluntary poverty or voluntary simplicity, letting go of excess stuff requires commitment and new skills.

Simplify, simplify, simplify. For many women, the thought of simplifying, economizing, and doing with less conjures up deep fears of scarcity and lack. We all want some measure of financial security. But what does it take to have that? Cheryl Richardson is a successful life coach and former tax consultant who helps women everywhere, from all walks of life, achieve successful life makeovers. In one of her Life Makeover e-newsletters on money, Richardson stresses that abundance flows when we trust ourselves enough to handle it. Abundance is our birthright, but the key to creating it lies in increasing our level of financial esteem. Her version of financial self-esteem includes the ability to feel good about how we handle what money we do have. She stresses three steps to financial self-esteem: build self-trust around handling money, shift your perspective to appreciating what you do have, and share your "wealth" (money, talent, experience) regardless of financial circumstances. Many women have a fear of success. Yet, you can redefine success right now as generosity, commitment, passion, full self-expression, and freedom. In *Your Money or Your Life*, Vicki Robin said, "I buy my freedom with my frugality."

Simple abundance—it is calming, cooling to the heart, mind, and senses, and doesn't clutter the road ahead. My Journal reflects on one of the stopping places on my journey.

*It pleases me to be in this place of simple abundance. The house is spacious enough that each person is accommodated graciously, with privacy, with just enough. The rhythm of home is felt here. There is a quality of lightness. I have enough private, alone time, and enough contact with others. I like being able to choose either based on my needs, my rhythms. After more than a year moving from place to place, forever gathering and un-gathering the necessities of my life, I sink into this simple abundance, let it hold and support me for awhile. In this stopping place I accept the now with gratitude.*

When I asked Voncille what is important for
other women to know about embarking on a similar
journey at midlife, she replied: "Financial security is
too high a high price to pay for a joyless life or living
a spiritual death." For Jacquie, it was important to
live the values of simplicity and sustainability in a
balanced ecological way. This meant leaving the
family home intact for holiday gatherings, taking
only what she really needed. In moving into her own
place, she acknowledged deep fear about her needs
being met. She watched herself clutching onto
things, and consciously remembered to let go. When
Mari left home, she completely ignored (or avoided)
the money issue and soon found herself with no
future resources. She has since found that simplicity
and frugality over the intervening years purchased
the freedom she now enjoys. Most of the women I
interviewed learned from their leaving home journey
that what they need always shows up if they trust
themselves and the basic goodness of the universe.

The women who shared their stories with me
were beautifully creative about housing. Much to her
adult children's dismay, Sophia swapped the family
home for a big green van that gave her mobility and
freedom, and safely met all her needs. Several women
made stopovers at spiritual communities, some found
that co-op housing met their needs for community
and connection. Others found house-sitting to be

advantageous. During my own leaving home journey, several long-term paid house-sitting jobs found me. Not only was I performing a service, but I found that house-sitting suited my needs at the time. Later I lived in a cooperative household. This worked for me because I had shared responsibility, community, no need for household possessions, was free to focus on rebuilding my psychology career, and it enabled me to save enough to buy my own home when I was ready.

Often, women are drawn to a service-orientation that allows them to live the feminine values of love, serenity, and spirit in action. Peace Pilgrim was one of the voluntary homeless women. At midlife she stripped away all remnants of her former identity, took the name of Peace Pilgrim, and walked for peace for three decades. She owned nothing, carried nothing, and accepted only gifts of sustenance. To do this required that she relinquish her ego needs, feelings of separateness, all attachments, and negative feelings. People who have met her remember her serenity and the intensity of her eyes. She was living what was for her a life of purpose and meaning. There is an organization called "RV-ing Women." This is a nationwide network of women who, having eschewed the traditional lifestyles of their earlier years, live and travel in an RV community year round. They have unique ways of supporting and communicating with each other. On my own three-month cross-country camping adventure with a six-year-old in tow, I learned I could trust myself and take risks. I rediscovered the simple goodness of life on the open road, found riches in the mountain wilderness, and serenity in the night sky. It didn't matter that I had no address or bank account, or that my home was a simple tent. My little boy was beside me, the air pure and clean, and I felt blessed. The skill is to let go of preconceived ideas about what is acceptable and to be creatively adventurous.

It takes enormous energy to go through any transition, especially at midlife when your values are changing and energy is waning. Being in transition and not knowing where you are headed requires a deeper level of self-trust, awareness and self-compassion than has ever been required of you. The perpetual challenge is to stay healthy in body, mind and spirit. And keep life simple.

## HEALTH MATTERS

Transition is an accelerated growth process during which things change and open more quickly than you ever imagined. You may find yourself flipping coins, tossing and turning at night, awash in anxiety and indecision. During chaotic times you can easily resonate with anxious others and become more chaotic—when what is required is a shift to a still, quiet energy. What feels chaotic in the moment is really a growth opportunity. The practical and spiritual work taking place is that of allowing yourself to feel vulnerable without contracting in fear. Nobody can be open and trusting when feeling fragmented, chaotic, or emotionally stressed by fear, clutching and grasping. For this reason alone there is a need for extra self-care.

Jacquie believes that self-care is every woman's spiritual issue. This is the woman who, for her sixtieth birthday, gave herself a sabbatical from her long-time role as family caretaker. It took three years for Jacquie to internally disengage from roles that drained her energy and kept her from being her authentic self. She worked valiantly at forgiveness and letting go of resentments and guilt. And then her husband died suddenly. Jacquie found herself reeling through yet another level of disorientation. "After taking care of the death details and selling the family home," she said, "I desperately needed to return to the things that ground me. I had physical energy, but no stamina. I'd been stretched too much by the part of me that wasn't authentic, that believed I still needed to be there for everybody. I could hold myself together through the day, but became a dishrag by day's end. I'd taken care of my chronically ill mother throughout my youth, so I decided early on that I'd never get sick. Now I must attend to my own health needs. This new level of transition has opened up a huge challenge to take better care of myself, to not ignore my own physical health needs."

Do you know where your energy drains are? Do you know how to prevent victimization? Your energy drains may be friends who don't support your authenticity, or junk mail and phone calls, or a demanding and unappreciative family member. Or outgrown roles like your own need to please. Maybe you habitually smile too much and now find it tiring. Perhaps there is repressed anger and conflicted emotions about being true to yourself. There may be unhealed physical or emotional trauma keeping you from caring for yourself. How do you respond to the needs of your body? Do you rely on coffee, alcohol, or medications to keep yourself energized? Do you take time to eat well and exercise regularly? Do you know your body's stress signals? Do you know how to receive emotional nourishment?

Neurotransmitters are chemical messengers that link our brain, peripheral nervous system, and immune system. They are the body's cellular communication system. For instance, gratitude and caring are known to be heart-centered needs. When the needs of the human heart are met, electromagnetic energy coming from the heart cells actually energizes all other cells of the body. The energetic vibrancy of living more authentically is in itself health-promoting. Research shows that trust and openness, as opposed to fear and limitation, actually promote stress reduction.

In addition to the spiritual benefits of meditation discussed in the last chapter, regular meditation contributes to a physically healthier you. More than a hundred health benefits of meditation have been demonstrated by research. Meditation not only increases stress resilience but it can reverse the bodily damage caused by stress. It energizes, improves sleep, restores a feeling of balance, improves concentration, decreases anxiety, and improves the function of the immune system. It creates a state of restful alertness, providing deep rest while the mind remains alert. There is solid evidence that meditation improves headaches, heart rhythm disturbances, blood pressure, and chronic pain. Immunity decreases normally with age as well as with sudden stress. Yet immune suppression has been proven to be reversible through simple meditation and relaxation exercises to shift the body out of stress mode. Meditation is healthy, safe and cheap. It is one of the best health investments you can make for yourself, and the benefits are cumulative with regular practice.

Women come alive at midlife. They often find a long-forgotten physical ability. They become long-distance bicyclists, weight lifters, marathon runners,

salsa dancers, yogis, kick-boxers, tai chi practitioners—and enjoy feeling their strength and caring for
their bodies.

Transition of any kind is inherently stressful, but
more so at midlife. Now is the time to implement
basic self-care strategies to protect your health. When
overwhelmed, do you tend to ignore self-care as you
push through your stress or pain threshold? As you
become aware of the stress signals your body gives you
every day, you'll find that your body can be your most
dependable friend. Learning to connect mind and
body enables you to make choices that honor your
physical, emotional, and spiritual health. Remember,
you don't have to do it alone. It is a myth that
women who dare to discard outworn roles and identities are alone, freakish, and unusual. Often, they are
stigmatized and misunderstood by loved ones and
society. The remedy is to break the silence and isolation, discard your shame, and talk. Tell your story,
speak your truth, dare to reach out for support.

## CONNECTION MATTERS

One of the hardest things about the midlife journey is that women who leave home at midlife are not
an identifiable group—they easily become invisible,
can't find others to connect with, and can become
isolated in this most difficult transition of their lives.
Women are relational beings by nature. Relationships

are the foundation of our health and happiness. They shape who we are and who we are becoming. They fill the emotional gaps in marriage and help us to remember we are really spiritual beings. The essential and health enhancing benefits of friendships between women have been demonstrated in a recent University of California (UCLA) study on women and stress. This groundbreaking research found that women respond to stress differently than men. This difference has significant health implications and may explain why women generally outlive men. The UCLA study, conducted by two women scientists, suggests that women respond to stress with an outpouring of brain chemicals that cause us to reach for and maintain connections with other women. It seems that when the hormone oxytocin is released as part of the female stress response, it buffers the ancient fight or flight response and encourages us to gather with children and other women and engage in nurturing and befriending behavior. This connecting behavior then releases more oxytocin, which further counters stress and produces a calming effect. This response does not occur in men. Men tend toward the well-known "fight or flight" behavior.

Research shows that friends help us live longer. Dean Ornish demonstrated that regardless of the cause of heart disease, social connectedness can help to renew the lining of the blood vessels which can reduce the risk of heart attack. Ohio State Medical School researchers found that lonely people had significantly lower levels of immunity than those who felt connected. Study after study has found that social ties reduce our risk of disease by lowering blood pressure, heart rate, and cholesterol. People who had the most friends over a nine-year period were found to have a sixty percent less risk of death. Studies have found that the more friends a woman has, the less likely she is to develop health problems as she ages (and the more likely she is to be living a joyful life). That's not all. Women with close friends and confidantes are more likely to cope with the death of a spouse without a loss of health and vitality. Those of you whose focus has primarily been work and career may now find that you haven't extended your social network to outside sources of friendship and support. It seems that every time we women get too busy with work, family or a new man, the first thing we do is let go of our female friendships. That's a mistake because these connections are a necessary source of strength, emotional nourishment, health, and healing.

During my research for this book, I asked women what sustained them on their leaving home journey. Elsie stressed the importance of kindred spirits. "Find fellow travelers," she said, "people who can support you and not judge the process you are going through." According to Voncille, "We must go where there is food for the soul and spirit—otherwise we are already dead. Find other women who have walked this road and spend more time with them." Jana confided, "I could not have made my transition without my women friends. Family or siblings would not have done what my women friends did. I would have just given up if not for their support. They saved my life, almost physically carried me across the threshold. If I can do that for other women, it would give me great joy." Ann said, "Get out there and ask for what you want and need, don't isolate, talk to people, network, get involved in women's groups. It's about allowing support and getting nurtured." Well said, ladies.

Networking is something most women do well. Yet, when feeling alone and helpless we don't always remember that support is available for the asking. One of my own personal lessons is that when I've befriended myself, people naturally respond to me, and the net keeps on working. It is by connection with kindred spirits that we build a sense of belonging, and recreate our lives and ourselves—sometimes over and over.

While the inner work of transition is being done there are practical issues to be faced daily that I hope this chapter has helped you to confront. You will be asked over and over to make challenging choices, so take the time right now to reflect on choices you've made in the past, as well as on your style of choice-making. An attitude of openness and self-trust is an important asset on this journey. As you grow in these areas, your attitude and self-esteem will be affected positively. As your attitude shifts, so will your ideas about success and abundance. You may even feel better about how you relate to money. Transition of any kind is stressful, but more so at midlife. Discover what drains your energy and implement self-care strategies that will protect your precious health and energy. It's your unique journey. You must do it alone, but you will want the support of kindred spirits. When feeling alone and helpless, reach out and connect with others on this path. Your work is to give birth to your authentic self and to meet the inevitable challenges along the way. Your life is your message. The next exercise is adapted from Martia Nelson. It can help you remember that support for both inner and outer work is essential for moving through transition.

## EXERCISE

1. Take time to sit quietly and let your breath take you inside. As you breathe, think or speak your intention to connect with your inner source of

support. Continue to bring your mind back to your intention to connect with this beautiful part of yourself.

2. Do whatever kind of movement (walk, jog, dance) that allows you to connect with the beauty of nature. As you move, repeatedly affirm aloud your intention to connect with your inner source of support.

3. Lastly, find a trusted friend with whom you can talk about your need for support. Exchange experiences. How do you maintain both inner and outer support? What does it feel like?

*The Gifts*

TEN

## Authenticity

*The game we play is let's pretend
and pretend we're not pretending.
We choose to forget who we are
and then forget that we've forgotten.*

—Bernard Gunther

Authenticity is a complex concept. It is neither defined nor experienced as neatly as a dictionary suggests. Similar to the model used in chapter 2 to explore inauthenticity, this chapter uses an Authenticity Symptom Checklist to demonstrate the multi-faceted nature of authenticity. This checklist is derived from the women's interview responses as well as from the e-survey I conducted asking people I knew and respected to share their current definition of authenticity. The linear checklist defining authenticity is then redrawn as the circular growth process it has been discovered to be by the actual women who have embarked on this journey. The very nature of spiritual growth is that there is no destination, just the freedom to BE.

Authenticity comes from the Latin *authenticus* and the Greek *authentikos*, which mean trustworthy, worthy of acceptance; not imaginary or false, but genuine and bona fide. The dictionary definitions include (1) worthy of belief, faithfulness to an original, authoritative, convincing, credible, faithful, true, trustworthy, valid; and (2) not counterfeit or copied, but genuine, good, original, real, unquestionable. Authenticity has both an objective and a subjective nature. It is used to describe bona fide material objects like antiques and art. However, for human beings authenticity is rather subjective because it is the act of living out a natural process of expansion. A process is not a linear event. Rather, it is an organic movement that tends to circle back into itself as it spirals forward or upward. Like a hurricane, the spiral seems chaotic, yet possesses a stable energy center that moves steadily toward an outcome.

We get root-bound and need repotting for growth. In *Something More*, Ban Breachnach says this repotting process begins when you admit that you want something more. The process involves peeling the layers of cultural conditioning to unearth the real you—that buried self, hidden by childhood wounds, the essence that was there before you took on a personality. By removing the accumulated psychological and emotional sediment and shedding what has kept you safe and predictable, you can unearth your authentic self. You accept who you are today, become your own soul friend, and begin making choices that honor your authenticity. This is the "something more" of which Ban Breachnach speaks.

Everything in life contributes to your soul's evolution. The way you respond to the inevitable difficulties on the path, to those scary places within, can help or hinder your growth. You can travel through life in the same old rut, or you can take the less-traveled road and cultivate the spiritual gifts that are your birthright. Spiritual work is not just a matter of repairing certain life situations. Rather, it has to do with restoring your connection to spirit. It is the disconnection from spirit that creates the false self. As you learned in chapter 8, any conscious move out of your comfort zone and into the scary places within, is a spiritual act. It empowers you to dive deep within and discover depths you didn't know you had. Whether you negotiate this journey physically, or metaphorically as Nancy and Karen did, you are asked to dig deep into your wellspring of truth and trust. Each time you do this you will retrieve a piece of your true self. So stop getting ready and allow whatever is calling. Give space to the you that is trying to be born.

Buddhist philosophy distinguishes between living in the *lower realms* and the *higher realms*. The lower realms refer to living purely for the sake of survival. This can mean living from basic instinct, as though your very survival depends on getting and consuming as much as you can; or living in constant fear from a poverty mentality; or with paranoia, denial, and guilt. All aspects of the lower realm are rooted in fear and self-doubt. The higher realms are marked by awareness, clarity, joy, freedom, and disciplined action. In Western thinking, the lower realms correlate with our shadow side as explained in chapter 5, while the higher realms correlate with openness, compassion, wholeness, and clarity—the qualities of authenticity. Chogyam Trungpa, the late Tibetan Buddhist teacher, taught that authentic presence is a spiritual virtue akin to a "field of power." He saw authentic presence as a natural process of expansion that is attained by discipline; by letting go of fixations such as attachment, doubt, fear, and hesitation; and by cultivating awareness and a belief in the basic goodness of life. To learn more about the Buddhist philosophy of authentic presence, I suggest *Shambhala: The Sacred Path of the Warrior* by Chogyam Trungpa.

Hameed Almaas was my spiritual teacher for almost ten years. He is a brilliant scholar who founded the Ridhwan School and the Diamond Approach to spiritual development. The school grew out of the needs of people leading ordinary contemporary lives who were seeking something more. Almaas has worked assiduously to integrate Western psychology and Eastern wisdom teachings. His approach is a straightforward form of moment-to-moment inquiry into one's direct experience, particularly the experience of emptiness that is so scary for most of us. Almaas teaches that when we digest the parts of the self we have split off or misunderstood, and do the arduous work of facing the personality with all its defenses, attachments, and identifications developed in childhood, we mature into the fullness of the authentic self. By understanding the process by which the inauthentic self is formed, we can then go to the next step and integrate ego into our spiritual nature. It is by disconnection from our spiritual nature that the inauthentic self is formed. Spiritual qualities of love, compassion, strength and clarity are recovered when we do the deep work of understanding and integrating personality with spiritual nature.

## SYMPTOMS OF AUTHENTICITY

When the urge to write about authenticity was calling me, I had the bright idea to do an e-survey. I did not yet trust my own wisdom and wanted fellow travelers to affirm what I already knew. So I sent a query to everybody in my personal address book, male and female alike, asking each one to share with me his or her current definition of authenticity. It was this generous and open sharing across cyberspace that enabled me to grasp the breadth and depth of authenticity. I gained deep respect for the complexity of our human journey, and especially for those who dug deep and stretched wide to share both the *what* and the *how* of becoming authentic. I want to share with you the wonderful, courageous, insightful responses. By far the most commonly used words were *truth* and *honesty*. Truth and honesty are related concepts, but with subtle differences. Both are within you. Speaking truth means having the capacity to say what is so for you without blame or judgment. Being honest means living by your own light, rather than by the opinions of others. My favorite definition comes from Bill, a former client with a poetic heart who said, "Authenticity is when the flame and shadow are one."

A librarian in love with words, Harry has this to say about authenticity: "Each person has a unique essence or true self and will naturally seek to become that essence. The problem is that none of us can identify what makes a person 'true' as opposed to 'false.' Authenticity is not a product of an active search because the conscious mind is dominated by a personal history and the imprint of social forces. Thus, authenticity is most closely approximated as we 'forget' ourselves and the conscious structuring of our lives. This forgetting not only undermines the social imprint, but the way by which we constantly create a self-image. This act of self-forgetting is the door to my authenticity, but I do not pass through a door, I simply note that passage is taking place and what emerges is a new layer of my authentic self. Others who note my authenticity do not see it per se, but they know me to be somehow genuine. To be authentic is to live out what is most true in me. Knowing this puts upon me the double burden that first, I must forget my small self and, second, that I must live without regard to structures and judgments placed upon me by myself and others. Thus, for human beings, authenticity is not what it is for material objects. Rather, it is a process by which we take on qualities that we comprehend primarily with the heart and spirit. Wow, all this! I had no idea when I started." Thank you, Harry, wherever you are.

In a somewhat different voice, Diana defines authenticity as a process. She provides insight into the *how* of the journey toward authenticity, rather than the *what*. *How* is a different question than *what* and is generally more useful. You may not need to change what you are doing; but it may be necessary to change how you are doing it. Diana says, "I am authentic when . . .

❖ I acknowledge my essential divinity
❖ I remember that I am loved, loving, and love
❖ I remember that I am not alone
❖ I am aware that I am part of something greater than I can imagine
❖ My actions reflect my goodwill
❖ I listen perceptively to others, refrain from judgment, and communicate honestly my personal truths and feelings
❖ I am kind and loving to myself and others
❖ I listen to the promptings of my soul
❖ I strive to act with integrity and in alignment with my personal values
❖ I allow my emotions to flow
❖ I honor and express my creativity."

In defining authenticity, Diana has clearly defined integrity. Integrity involves speaking your truth, saying what is so without blame or judgment. It is being all of one piece—body, mind, spirit. Have you noticed a gap between your values and the way you live those values through your words, deeds and intentions? When you reduce that gap you have gained integrity. To live with integrity means having your actions reflect your deepest values, rather than saying one thing and doing something else. A few questions to consider right now: Do you listen to your inner voice? Do your actions express your values? Can you speak honestly without abandoning your ideas or feelings, yet be open to others?

SELF-RESPONSIBILITY ∽ Deanna responded to my e-survey by addressing the importance of self-responsibility. She says, "Authenticity means knowing myself. It is my willingness to reveal my true self to others—warts and all. I speak easily (but appropriately) of my vulnerabilities as well as strengths, of my feelings toward another, especially when those feelings are positive. Being authentic is doing the work I love, even if it must be an avocation due to financial constraints or responsibilities to others. I explore avenues of self-expression to which I feel drawn, striving to develop myself to the fullest by testing my innate abilities, yearnings, and desires. I believe we are each happiest, most fulfilled, most authentic when we are stretching, growing, evolving in directions in which we feel pulled or propelled. This includes living according to the teachings of our chosen spiritual path." Deanna responded at length about the danger of confusing being authentic with being rude, inconsiderate, tactless and insensitive to others, reminding us of the importance of self-responsibility. She stressed the importance of "being true and honest to oneself, while keeping the perspectives and concerns of others in mind." This suggests that self-responsibility is a key quality of authenticity.

Self-responsibility is having the courage to live your own values while at the same time valuing relationships. Not an easy task! By making choices that enhance the quality of your life and nurture your dreams, you are living with integrity. Your ability to make choices with integrity is inextricably linked to self-worth. As a self-responsible person you communicate in ways that consider the right timing, place, and context of the situation. You speak your truth without blame or judgment, saying what you see and feel with compassion. Having the ability to be both honest and compassionate is a good indicator that you are being authentic. None of us live in a vacuum. Rather, we live in an interdependent web of existence. As you move toward greater authenticity and self-determination, you naturally become more self-responsible on all levels.

"My soul was dying." "My spirit had died." "I needed to save my life." You will recall that each of the women I interviewed reported some version of spiritual death that prompted her home-leaving journey. Each was experiencing a profound disconnection from her true self. They each bought the stereotype that being good or loving meant stifling her desire for truth. We are not meant to stop and lay fallow, give up, and not thrive in this life. We have the responsibility to wake up to what is needed in order to continue to evolve spiritually. We are each called again and again to wake up. Once we heed that wake up call we can never get back on the same horse again. There is disappointment in the ways of the small self. Difficult choices and consequences present themselves again and again. Yet you don't have to wait for life to rudely awaken you in order to reclaim the unique person you already are. Awakening is a gradual process leading to integration, wholeness, and spiritual maturity that is best seen as a process rather than a fixed destination.

How often do you find yourself looking to others for fulfillment and purpose, instead of taking responsibility for your own experience and your own needs? Nothing and nobody in the future will rescue you or make you happy. Your truth will not be found in the opinions and belief systems of others. It can, however, be found in the stillness within you. To get to that stillness all you have to do is stop, listen to your authentic voice, and be present to what *is*.

PRESENCE ∽ Presence is power. It is *your* authentic power. Presence means you are willing and able to show up mentally, physically, spiritually and emotionally; you are wide awake, senses fully open, and there is no filter between you and your experience. An added bonus is that you are more likely to recognize your inner guidance when you are present. When you can take responsibility for your own experience in each situation, you will have gained a sweet dominion over yourself. Are you a person who chases activity, material things, physical appearance, looking good? If so, you are living through your false self by avoiding being present. This may be a good time for you to re-read chapter 8. Your life can be different by choosing to change your choices. You can change your choices by recognizing what is true in each moment.

In chapter 1 we saw how withdrawing into neutral is a way of emotionally leaving what you can't change. Withdrawing into neutral is the polar opposite of being present. It constitutes alienation from self and the world. Is it safer to stay in neutral and be gray and numb? No! In neutral you are disconnected from your senses, akin to being asleep and unconscious. You do not see what is there to be seen because you are numb to what is. This is a dreadful form of self-betrayal. What turns hard and rigid in the human psyche is more easily shattered. To be a victim of life is a choice, not a requirement. The key to true freedom lies in how you choose to experience your life, rather than in the externals. The externals are not who you are, but the result of who you are.

In writing *The Key*, Cheri Huber has provided us with an excellent primer about presence and the importance of being in the now. Huber stresses that life happens only in the present moment, in the now. The past is gone, the future is not yet here. There is only now. How you think about yourself and your life actually shapes it. Being intentional and thoughtful requires more time, but results in more conscious action on your part. When you are disconnected from the present moment, where is your energy? It is probably not available to you, and authentic presence cannot blossom. Huber counsels that there is nothing to understand before you can become present. Presence itself is the key. Wherever you are, be there fully, with all your senses open. Stop, look and listen to your experience in the moment. Being present reconnects you with your natural longing for balance and wholeness. Honor the present moment by standing open to it, listening to the silence within, giving full attention to your experience in the moment, and fully accepting what is. This will bring you home to your authentic self—the only true success in this life.

AWARENESS ∞ Awareness is a gift of presence and, simultaneously, presence is a gift of awareness. Both are aspects of higher consciousness that point the way toward what the mystics call enlightenment, or finding our light. When you are fully aware, all your senses, feelings, thoughts, sensations, and intuition are activated. You are awake and more able to discern truth and reality. You are also grounded in the body. Body awareness will always keep you present. Right now, try shifting your awareness from your thinking mind to your body. For just this moment, can you sense into your arms, your legs, the energy field of your body? Do you notice a sense of being "indoors" that is qualitatively different from when you are solely dominated by your thoughts? Chapter 8 offers several time-honored practices for being more aware and present in your life. You may find yourself saying, "But I don't have time to pay attention; I'm too busy to practice being aware." That's okay, as long as you remember who is making that choice, and who is responsible for your experience.

SELF-COMPASSION ∞ One of the qualities you have the opportunity to develop at midlife and beyond is more compassion for yourself. Women typically find it easier to feel compassion for others, but can be harsh and unforgiving with themselves. There are two reasons for this. First, women are by nature relational beings and, second, we have been socialized to be nice girls, to put others first and ourselves last. For many women, being a nice girl has taken the form of self-neglect: neglect of our needs, desires, truth, and our soul. We have been taught to have compassion for others, but few of us have been taught to have compassion for ourselves. Midlife is the time to resolve this split between self-neglect and self-compassion. Self-compassion is a quality of the heart, and it is your birthright. Heartfelt forgiveness of your mistakes in the present and your wounds of the past is a compassionate act. If you find this difficult to do, think of the loving kindness you have felt toward a little child or other loved ones, or times when you have been touched by another's compassion toward you. Self-compassion is that same loving kindness given to yourself.

Martia Nelson, in *Self-Compassion: Secret to Spiritual Success*, describes self-compassion as " . . . a gentle state because it is so subtle and quiet, and it is a warrior's state because it is so powerful for making life changes." She offers the following exercise to give yourself the experience of self-compassion.

## EXERCISE

Take a moment to close your eyes, and with each of your next three breaths, silently say the following words: "Sweet me." Then do it again, this time looking gently for the most microscopic sensations of sweetness emanating through you. Then do it once more, opening to the tiniest sweetness for yourself. Whenever you are worried, hurt, frightened or angry, allow "Sweet Me" to bring your emotions back into balance. Nelson calls self-compassion "the most powerful tool for transformation you might ever find. It is having sweetness for yourself, no matter what else you might be experiencing."

The media have given much attention lately to the "daughter track." The daughter track is the modern label for an age-old, compassionate, women's response that is now being ascribed to professional women of the baby-boomer generation who are giving up careers and sometimes moving across the country to care for aging parents. The question becomes, how can the caregiver have compassion for herself? Judy Payne is a midlife woman who shared with me her simple, heartfelt poem about her own struggle to find compassion for herself as the caretaker of a loved one.

How can the caregiver care for herself? Where does she draw the strength?

How long can the caregiver deny her own needs, before she can't go the length?

How can the caregiver care for herself, with husband, grandkids and mom in tow?

How long will it take 'till her spirit breaks down, and her loved ones become the foe?

Are the answers obvious to all but herself, her solutions hidden in fog?

Or has the slow leak of her essence and wealth drained spirit, while carrying others through bog?

She calls on the Goddess, screaming out her own name, drawing strength from her center. And when she is done,

*Renewed spirit fans her own flame.*
*She lays down the burdens and turns toward the Sun.*

A study by Mark Leary, a Wake Forest University psychologist, revealed that self-compassion helps people cope with failure. In fact, it is more important than high self-esteem in coping with negative life events. This study found that highly self-compassionate people actually took more responsibility for their shortcomings and problems, they didn't beat themselves up when things went badly, and they were able to admit their mistakes. The study suggests that some of the positive responses to failure and rejection credited in the past to high self-esteem may really be credited to self-compassion. Self-compassion may be particularly beneficial for those with low self-esteem and for people who are excessively self-focused. When you gift yourself with acceptance and loving kindness for all that you are, warts and all, you will come out of your self-neglect and abandonment into the light of your authentic self. Self-rejection keeps you stuck in self-neglect and the related negative emotions. If you bring this gentle quality of self-compassion to your own soul, to its wounded and exiled places, you will find deep inner healing. What do you need to change in order to feel more self-compassion? What keeps you from choosing to change?

The more aware you become of the price you

pay when you are not being your true self, the more likely you are to choose to change. Here are some suggestions for developing the self-compassion and self-responsibility that can transform your difficult feelings and situations.

## EXERCISE

First, think of something in your life that isn't going as well as you would like—health, parenting, career, a personal relationship. Then explore what there is about that situation that is difficult for you. For instance, your health is suffering from work-related stress. Your habitual pattern has been to criticize yourself for suffering the effects of a stressful job, thinking you are somehow deficient, and then to push yourself harder. What quality can you bring to this unhealthy situation? Self-compassion can help, as can forgiveness for neglecting your own needs and risking a stress-related illness. Try creating a phrase that would reinforce your intention to change, while at the same time acknowledging that you don't yet know how to embrace this missing quality. For example, try "While I haven't known how to have compassion for myself, starting right now I'll practice self-compassion at every opportunity." To practice, do the "Sweet Me" meditation described above. Try to experience yourself filled with the sweetness of self-compassion (or any quality you would like to develop). The idea is to imagine what it would feel like to have compassion for yourself, then to experience the sense of well-being that comes from treating yourself with gentle, loving kindness. The more you practice, the easier it will be to experience this or any other personal quality when you need it.

∽

I hope you now recognize that authenticity is a complex concept that is not easily defined or experienced. When traveling the path that is the focus of this book, you are asked to employ your highest resources by going deep within and reclaiming neglected or abandoned qualities. This brings you closer to living your deepest truth and values with responsibility and compassion. Developing awareness of what is most true and valued requires being present, noticing what is. The practice of presence will allow wholeness and balance to blossom in your life and relationships. Self-compassion is essential for living authentically. As women, we have not been told we can have compassion for ourselves, nor have we been taught how to cultivate this essential quality. This wound underlies the depression, anxiety and addictions so many women struggle with at midlife. I conclude this chapter with an Authenticity Symptom Checklist to help guide you on your journey to authentic self. The linear list of symptoms is then redrawn to represent the multi-layered spiral of growth that it really is.

## AUTHENTICITY SYMPTOM CHECKLIST

_____ Acting and speaking from an inner directedness

_____ Experiencing congruence between inner and outer

_____ Living consciously from inner wisdom

_____ Trusting my intuitive guidance

_____ Inhabiting my own soul with peace and unabashed honesty

_____ Feeling good in my own skin

_____ Being me as fully as I can

_____ Knowing my values and consciously living them

_____ Being without mask or facade, not hiding who I am

_____ Being me without apology or explanation

_____ Growing in directions in which I am pulled or propelled

_____ Claiming the rightness of what I need for health, fulfillment, and joy

_____ Experiencing the absence of self-deception

_____ Taking responsibility for my own wants and needs

_____ Knowing and expressing myself with grace and compassion

_____ Communicating my truth while respecting others

_____ Listening to and responding compassionately to my true feelings

_____ Speaking my personal truth about my beliefs and values

_____ Living from my deepest truth, as best I can know it

_____ Experiencing the process of waking up

_____ Living my spiritual wisdom

_____ Knowing myself as God

_____ Experiencing the flame and shadow as one

_____ _____

_____ _____

_____ _____

FREEDOM

SPIRITUAL MATURITY
AUTHENTICITY
INNER AUTHORITY
WHOLENESS
TRUST - PRESENCE
AWAKENING
SEEING TRUTH - ACCEPTANCE
COMPASSION
COURAGE
AWARENESS
STANDING STILL - STANDING OPEN

## ELEVEN

# Freedom

*Knowing what you know,*
*Knowing what you don't know,*
*Knowing what you are doing,*
*Then you have freedom to choose.*

—Kati Pressman

There are many spiritual paths and each in its own way asks you to stop, look, and listen. Spirituality is about your relationship to you—it doesn't matter whether your role model is Jesus, Mother Mary, Buddha, or Mohammed. A path to spiritual freedom is one that helps to deepen awareness, develop compassion, and increase your ability to be present with what is. Any practice that facilitates unity of body, mind and spirit will lead to spiritual freedom. Freedom in this sense means to have achieved integration, glimpsed wholeness, and tasted authenticity.

## BALANCE

Finding balance between inner and outer is a developmental task for all humans. We all have the ability to bring our fragmented selves into greater balance. This involves befriending and integrating the disowned parts of the self—the shadow side, discarding outworn roles and beliefs, and ultimately finding a balance between the inner and outer. For most midlife women, this means balancing the need for independence with the feminine need for relationships. When in balance we can more easily hold opposites, embrace reality with compassion, and strive to be open to what is. In other words, we can experience equanimity, inner peace, and acceptance.

I have often observed in my clinical practice that when a person's inner and outer life is out of balance, daily functioning is affected in subtle and profound ways. Work or personal relationships become driven by insecurity and fear. A person might find herself besieged by anger or greed. She may be haunted by indecisiveness, rebellion, or submissiveness—unresolved emotional qualities from childhood.

Even if your outer life looks successful, neglecting the inner can be hazardous. Without an inner life, you lose the ability to access your inner knowing and to regulate your precious life force. Stress mounts, personal relationships deteriorate, your health suffers, and you become vulnerable to looking to outer sources for stimulation—such as drugs or alcohol, competition, a new lover, or worse. You can become more vulnerable to disabling stressors such as anxiety and depression.

Paying attention to your inner life builds self-awareness and wholeness. You can start with a daily meditation, prayer, yoga, or tai chi practice to increase mindfulness, inner calm, and stress resilience. Spend time in nature. Connect with a fellowship or community that supports your spiritual growth. Cultivate the positive emotions of compassion and connectedness. Engage in physical exercise. Find a way to be of meaningful service to others to cultivate generosity of spirit and gratitude. It is not our material stuff that brings freedom. Rather, freedom is the awareness that true abundance lies within.

## WITNESSING

All worldly events can be expressed as pairs of opposites, or polarities: light and dark, up and down, love and hate, good and bad. This is simply the way it is. Many religious approaches attempt to work with polarities by suppressing one side—using the sledgehammers of dogma, or morality, or willpower. Life lived from only one side of a polarity requires a great deal of energy to push away the denied reality of its opposite. Carl Jung noticed that whatever we artificially push out of awareness will continually reemerge in our lives until we notice and work to integrate it. Until then, life can be needlessly difficult or shallow.

I remember with fondness an experience from my tenure as a spiritual life trainee at Kripalu Center for Yoga and Health. Kripalu at that time expected its primarily American spiritual seekers to abide by some inordinate cultural polarities: yogic celibacy, separation of the sexes, a six and a half day work week, and a diet consisting of vegetables, rice, beans, fruits, nuts, and bancha tea, with popcorn for dessert on Wednesday nights. I remember with delight the nights we stole out of the ashram and silently drove to the far edge of town where a bona fide old-fashioned ice cream parlor awaited. Here I would sit at the Formica counter and greedily gulp a cup of real coffee with a scoop of luscious vanilla ice cream floating in it. And just as silently we'd later slip back into the ashram feeling like wickedly delighted kids. I had never been in the habit of coveting coffee or ice cream in the middle of the night until my freedom to embrace the polarities of ice cream and spiritual life was denied me.

ENDINGS. BEGINNINGS . . .

We suffer when we try to separate what are really two ends of the same spectrum. There is a technique from Eastern spiritual philosophy that is remarkably useful for working with polarities. It is called developing the *witness consciousness*—the capacity to objectively experience things as they are, without tuning out or denying opposites. The witness is the awake part of you, the clear head at your center that is capable of standing still, even in the midst of emotional chaos, without censoring or judging or reacting. It does not choose for or against any aspect of reality. It just notices.

At one point in my psychology training I facilitated women's domestic violence groups. Week after week I listened to stories of conflict and abuse and at times felt I could bear no more—of the stories, or of my own dismay, anger and angst. I felt deep compassion for these women who didn't know how to find their way out of relationship abuse. I was furious at a social system that looked the other way. The following year, however, I found myself conducting men's domestic violence groups. I was afraid at first. And I was judgmental, having defined the women as victims, the men as perpetrators, polarizing them into extremes of good and bad. Then I listened to the stories of these men's lives, of childhood abuse and abandonment. Their shame was palpable. I also learned that much of the men's childhood physical abuse was perpetrated by their mothers. Again I felt compassion. Their mothers were victims of a multi-generational cycle of abuse perpetrated by fathers, brothers, uncles, and neighbors on little girls. As adults they all lived out what they knew. At some point I was able to hold both the women and the men with compassion and equanimity, seeing both as part of an inter-generational cycle of abuse whereby all are victims.

Stephen Cope, in *Yoga and the Quest for the True Self*, describes witnessing as "the primary skillful means for freeing us from our bondage." In this sense, bondage means the yo-yo effect of craving and aversion, good and bad, right and wrong. When we recognize that the pairs of opposites are not separate, that they are one, we develop the capacity to experience the way things are, to live each moment more fully and without judgment. Cope calls this "riding the wave." He describes five steps to riding the wave.

❖ The first step is to breathe, allowing the life force to fill your body.

❖ Second, relax muscle tension in your body because it blocks the flow of energy, feeling, and sensation. It is best to begin by relaxing the belly. As the wave of breath and energy builds in intensity, you may tense up to defend against it.

❖ The third step is to allow your feelings, letting sensation move into any emotions that arise.

❖ The fourth step is to pay attention to your moment-to-moment experience, without judgment or analyzing it.

❖ Finally, resist the temptation to "fix" anything. Simply observe and allow what is, letting your experience touch you, just as it is, without resistance or the need to change it. It's okay to not understand it. Just let it happen

The purpose of riding the wave is to look deeply at what is running your life. With practice, it can lead to developing the witness consciousness described above. You can trust the natural process to support you as you move toward greater integration, balance, and wholeness.

## WHOLENESS

Particularly for the midlife woman, there is a hunger for completion that often comes in the form of a calling, a shout or a whisper—beckoning her to shed roles that have kept her out of balance. This inner call is always growth-motivated, a call to self-knowledge and truthful self-expression. I remember poignantly my first night living at Esalen Institute. Each of us in my fledgling work-scholar group was asked to say why we were there. Without thinking I said, "To find wholeness." I had no conscious understanding of what that meant; and I was surprised to hear the words. Now I know it was my spontaneous expression of a midlife call to integration. My years at Esalen were fertile ground for my healing and the integration that led to this book. Still, many years would pass before I would fully understand this natural impulse, this hunger for oneness within and without. We each possess an innate drive for the aliveness that is our birthright. All spiritual traditions embrace the concept of wholeness, that natural impulse for unity rather than separateness. The ancient symbol of yin and yang depicts the harmonious whole that lies beyond male-female stereotypes that cripple us. To become spiritually mature, we are asked to find the wholeness that is beyond male and female roles.

We each long for wholeness, yet seek it in different ways. There are difficult choices to be made along the way—letting go of outworn habits and relationships, small deaths of the ego, and facing the obstacles within and without as we move toward living more authentically. When Elsie said in chapter 8, "We're not a piece of God. We are each wholly God," she meant that wholeness is when we experience ourselves as part of a much larger reality. This is spiritual freedom. It is when the flame and shadow are one. It has been said that everything in life follows a circular process. The real question is whether the circles of our growth become smaller or larger, whether they are closing down or opening to a greater inclusiveness, whether or not there is movement toward wholeness.

Growth is a dynamic process, a journey *toward*. It is a gradual process with no shortcuts, and change is the only reliable constant. Sometimes growth creeps up on us without our realizing it, and other times we are right in it, having an *ah-ha* experience. It is a process unique to each person that reveals the wonder and mystery of spiritual growth. We move toward wholeness when life experiences are consistently integrated, chewed up and digested. For women at midlife, what asks to be integrated is all that has been fragmented by living in a society that dishonors feminine values.

Integration has to do with *integrity*—being all of one piece, walking your talk, acting from your deepest values—rather than trying to make nice. If you act with integrity you don't have to fear that being yourself means you won't care for others because, by definition, being in integrity means you will treat others with care, compassion, and love. It is no mistake that the current psycho-spiritual movement described by Paul Ray in chapter 7 is comprised largely of midlife women and is dubbed the *integral culture*. Women are awakening together and sending a message of hope, health, and healing. Such an exquisite gift! The following is an excerpt from my leaving home journal.

*Since leaving home I have recovered the ability to know what does and does not feel okay to me. I see more clearly when people try to control me, disrespect my*

*needs and wishes, and how I have allowed that to contin-
ue. I've reclaimed the capacity to discriminate that I lost
during my years in relationship. My instincts are sharp-
ened. Awareness of my needs and feelings is heightened.
I was so profoundly out of touch with my true nature
that I didn't even know how abusive I was to myself by
staying in what wasn't working for me, both professionally and personally. I feel daily a deep gratitude for my
renewed capacity to trust myself. I am in awe of the gifts
I have received by trusting my leaving home journey. The
greatest gift is gratitude for my life, my friends, and my
ability to trust that my journey is leading me to greater
good. I am saying yes to life. I have the courage to walk
toward life, rather than away from it. By saying yes to
life, I can accept my losses with the openness of a child
and the grace of an adult.*

## SPIRITUAL MATURITY

Saying yes to life is the starting point of spiritual
maturity. Living a balanced life is spiritual maturity.
As with any other passage in life, we can seek encouragement and support from others, but in the end the
yes has to come from within. Making this commitment to life happens naturally when we have achieved
a level of self-acceptance and compassion. Only after
we have experienced the darkness of the false self does
our choice to live more authentically gain real meaning. Then there begins an upward spiral of growth

that culminates in the wisdom, integrity and freedom that characterize spiritual maturity. Much has been said about the human qualities of spiritual maturity, a dialogue that spans most of the mainstream religious traditions, Eastern spiritual philosophies, and psychological perspectives. The major difference among the opinions seems to be whether spiritual authority resides within the individual, or whether it comes from an external source. The brand you follow doesn't matter as much as how your commitment to personal truth and integrity is expressed in your life.

The root meaning of *spiritual* comes from the Latin *spiritus*, which means *breath*, as in breathing. Ancient cultures and many Eastern mystical philosophies believe that the essence of life is breath. Also, the Hebrew word *ruach* means both breath and spirit. The basic meaning of spirit is not something supernatural, but rather the abundance that is in each of us. Fulfillment of our human potential is spirituality. Spirituality is an aspect of life that connects us with our deeper selves and with the world. It deepens and uplifts us, empowers and transforms us to live our lives with more integrity, effectiveness, serenity, and hope. It does not pull us out of life, but gives meaning and purpose to life by drawing together body, mind, and emotions into a harmony we call spirit.

Cathy is the minister you met in chapter 5. She generously shared her current understanding of spiritual maturity. "Growing into spiritual maturity takes intention, discipline, and a lifetime of work. We can learn from many of the world religions about spiritual maturity. Each has a truth and each, being human constructions, falls short of full truth. While we can learn something about who we are from all religions, it takes learning and practice and a commitment to the free and responsible search for truth and meaning. This means a desire for truth at all costs, which demands an open mind. It doesn't happen by accident. A discipline of meditation can help to develop wisdom and compassion as we learn to see ourselves and life more clearly. The Christian scriptures teach about abundant living, and that the fruits of the spirit are love, joy, peace, patience, goodness, gentleness and self-control. The Hebrew Bible teaches about learning to say yes again and again to what life brings. Taoism teaches us flexibility. The *Tao te Ching* teaches that there are only three spiritual qualities: simplicity, patience, and compassion. All religious and spiritual traditions agree that spiritual growth is intentional and requires a commitment to grow, and that it is a gradual process of development with no shortcuts." Well said.

Spiritual growth is not a linear journey. There is an inevitable succession of growth stages that create a more authentic life. The early developmental psychologists, Jung, Erikson, and Maslow, defined human development as an evolution from false self to true self, from inauthenticity to authenticity. This evolution is a lifelong journey of individuation and self-actualization, moving toward wholeness and ending in death, the final stage of development. The later stages of human development are characterized by the attainment of integrity, meaning, and wisdom. Through these continual acts of transformation a person attains the wisdom of spiritual maturity.

Nancy, whom you met in chapter 1, has had a spiritual practice of daily yoga and meditation and an affiliation with a spiritual teacher for thirty years, so I asked her to share her views on spiritual maturity at this stage of her life. She responded, "For me, spiritual maturity is the ability to be true to myself, instead of trying to be someone else. This involves self-acceptance, which for me began when 'trying' became too strenuous, and then the realization of the futility of trying. This realization came into the picture simultaneously with a greater sense of humor, acceptance of the mistakes I make, and a greater self-love. Having an ongoing practice has led me to the conclusion that I am God. And you. And you. And all of us. This is a gradually opening curtain, and I don't know it all the time, but my awareness of that presence gets greater as time passes and as I get older. Therefore, there is less to fear. I am really glad for that. There is no time to waste in fighting, but there is also no time for not being truthful. So words must be chosen carefully. I choose my battles, and most of them aren't worth fighting. No time. Self-acceptance leads to acceptance of others. Criticism of self leads to criticism of others. Loving kindness, patience, and compassion are what I ask for every day.

"When I turned fifty I asked Babaji, my teacher of thirty years, if all this new clarity was a result of my daily practice or the maturing process. He laughed. Daily practice was the answer. I know now that it is both of these, not one without the other. For years I was afraid of Babaji. Now I see him as one of my closest and wisest friends. I think being afraid had to do with shame, being ashamed of myself and all my parts. As my self-acceptance grew, so did our friendship. Although I don't see him very much anymore, he is part of me.

"One morning a few years ago I woke up realizing that my time left to do 'it' (become enlightened, which really isn't the goal anymore, and I'm not sure I even have a goal anymore) was getting short, so I gave up wanting it. If I grow to something I don't know about yet, lovely; and if this is it, this is good enough. It's not that I gave up striving, as I still want to be a kind and good person—but the complexion has changed, and I don't have the energy to work at this, so I'm letting myself be. I'm learning to laugh more. I am grateful to have had this practice as a daily anchor, and I believe in the process completely."

Nancy continues, "The cycles of spiritual growth lead us from without to within. At first we take as absolute authority the words of a teacher (or church). And so we become sheep, and do the practice, and quote the teacher, and basically give up ourselves. But doing so eventually leads us back to ourselves. I'm not sure when this happens, but it seems to happen when we start to question belief systems. And then you realize that the truth can only be found within. Which is what my teacher has said from the start. Babaji has said numerous times that he, the teacher, is only a projection of ourselves. Right now I'm looking at the inner authority. What exactly is it, and who is doing the looking? What an interesting quandary. So then I just go back to breath in, breath out. Because that may be all there is to it. The rest is just how we pass the time. Life is really juicy and much better than I would have ever dreamed. I am very grateful."

We have choices all along the way. The very nature of human existence is a continual cycle of change. Each cycle we encounter gives way to the next stage of growth. As consciousness and awareness grow, as we move upward through the spiral of growth, we begin to notice the choices we are making. How can you best honor both your choices and your life situation? How can you be true to yourself and true to the natural unfolding of your life? The following story tells how one woman navigated choice and disillusionment on her way to spiritual maturity.

JEAN ∽ Jean was sixty years old when she told me her story. Her journey is a living example of how the cycles of spiritual growth can express themselves in a woman's life. I was not surprised to learn that she had twice been a Roman Catholic nun, but evidently others had found this fact to be either amusing or bewildering. Jean doesn't fit the stereotypical nun image that was portrayed by Audrey Hepburn in "The Nun's Story," or Whoopi Goldberg in "Sister Act," or Sally Field in "The Flying Nun." She emanates equanimity, authenticity and peace. She is a lesbian. Jean described her spiritual journey as the story of the ugly duckling: a struggle to fit in, to be accepted for who she is. As a child her physical appearance did not reflect her Italian-Spanish roots. As a teenager her liberal social, political, and religious views did not reflect those of her traditional, conservative family. In the era in which Jean was raised, there were only two viable life choices for a woman born into an Italian-Catholic family: the first was marriage to a Catholic man in order to have sufficient children to fill the church pews; the second was joining the religious life of God's chosen few in order to minister to the families in the pews. Somewhere way down the line of life choices was being single, but these were the women who must, it was whispered, have something wrong with them.

Although Jean enjoyed a normal social life growing up, she said, "I was not comfortable with the male/female roles and expectations. I was enthralled with the nuns who were my school teachers, those well-educated women who seemed to have a real purpose in life. They seemed to live a peaceful and harmonious life together. There was a bond between them and a strong sense of belonging to a community. There was support, companionship, encouragement, group effort toward a common goal, a chosen family. I felt drawn to be one of them. There also seemed to be something very mysterious about them—a certain something that made them seem almost ethereal, other worldly, yet very grounded and focused on the earth."

Jean entered the convent at age fourteen, and for the next ten years she struggled to reconcile her idealized image of convent life with the reality of her struggle to fit in, to feel confirmed in her choice to be a nun. Some of her superiors had problems with her openness, honesty and questioning. She would have her ups and downs, doubts and insights, good days and not so good days. She continued to pray, to teach, and to work at being in community with the sisters. By her tenth year, major changes had occurred in church policy and nuns were given more freedom—freedoms that were being questioned within the community of nuns themselves. Jean said, "My questioning of the teachings, which originally had been considered evidence of my interest and dedication, was now viewed as an attack on the authority of my superiors. My spontaneity was being blocked, my creativity aborted; I felt like I was drying up." Jean looked for and found little support from her community. She felt betrayed. To think of leaving the convent to which she'd given ten years of her life was tantamount to divorce. Her discouragement and disillusionment grew to despair. She considered suicide to escape the pain. Jean entered the convent at fourteen and left the first time when she was twenty-four.

What was calling Jean to leave her convent home the first time? "I didn't know I was a lesbian at the time I left. Church disapproval was so strong I'd repressed my sexual orientation. I just knew I needed to be free to be me. I wanted affirmation that my thinking was okay. There was a heavy overlay of self-criticism and emotional conflict. I felt angry, betrayed and embarrassed. Even my mother questioned me. The outsider feeling which I had experienced early on in regard to my family and social life as a teenager, was the same feeling that drove me from the community of women where I had thought I belonged."

Jean felt a profound disillusionment and loss of identity when she left the convent that first time. It was not what she had imagined it would be. In her youthful longing for connection and community, Jean had idealized the nuns' purpose and role. After she left the convent she taught school, earned a graduate degree, and became a clinical occupational therapist—all the while pulling the pieces together professionally, but still looking for her soul community. Something spiritual was missing from her life. Her sexual orientation was put on the back burner, so to speak, and she had no romantic relationships. Meanwhile, her sister came out as a lesbian and while others seemed to recognize Jean's sexual orientation, she did not. Her longing for service and community was still strong ten years after leaving the convent and rejecting all participation in religious life.

About this time in her journey Jean found a liberal Catholic church where she could speak her mind, and there she began to feel nourished personally and spiritually. At age forty-four, after a twenty-year absence, Jean returned to the convent and to the same order of sisters. What was different? She was! But in less than three years, at age forty-seven, Jean left the convent a second time. This time the leaving was quite different. She had realized that the question was not, "How could I think of leaving?" Rather, it was "How could I think of staying?" Once she'd asked the right question she was free, and there was no experience of loss or letting go. "As I was putting on my veil one morning, I looked in the mirror and woke to the truth that this was not the community of women to which I was being called. The community to which I was being called was the community of lesbians. That was the community of my soul." Jean had listened to her intuition, found her truth, and chose to live with her choice without guilt. She wanted to explore life, to find her true self, and live authentically. This was not something she'd been taught in the convent. She reflected, "In looking back, I realized I was looking outside myself to belong. The truth is I found myself by looking within. I belong to myself and to who I am. And that is what I can bring to a community. There is no struggle, no doubt, no disappointment with this discovery—just peace and calm." Jean continues her work in her chosen field and has been in a mature, loving, committed relationship with a woman for ten years.

I asked Jean about the gifts of her journey. She affirms that she has found real joy, that her life is good and positive. She also knows that life is too short and nothing lasts forever, so claiming and living her joy is a gift. Jean rejected the letter of the law, so to speak, in favor of integrity. She reminds us, "If it is not true for you, it's not mature. You can't swallow anything on faith, you must digest it for yourself. It's about you and your relationship to you. The life and message of both Jesus and Ghandi have become part of my truth. Jesus said, 'The kingdom of God is within you.' Spiritual maturity is your truth revealed in your actions. Once truth is seen, if not acted on, it represents living a lie. It has to do with the way you are in relationship to yourself and others. It is your moment-to-moment experience being lived out with integrity; it comes at all ages, is a process, and never a done deal." Jean finds that her choices have been good, she has meaningful work that has a positive impact on others. And she has found beauty in her authentic self, which she defines as "having integrity about who I am and feeling comfortable with how I live my values."

Jean's story affirms that we can trust our own truth regardless of what that looks like to others. What does she want other women to know about embarking on a similar journey at midlife? That it takes courage to step into the unknown and to trust there is a path that will take you home. And that the journey to true self is an upward spiral leading to awakening. And we spiral through the same places in ourselves again and again, leaving the familiar in order to find it anew. Each time we pass through the spiral we achieve a measure of integration, wholeness, and authenticity. This has been Jean's journey toward spiritual maturity.

Jack Kornfield is a respected Buddhist meditation teacher, author, and clinical psychologist who describes the qualities of spiritual maturity in *A Path with Heart*. He teaches that spiritually mature people "have a sense of life's irony, metaphor, and humor, and a capacity to embrace the whole, with its beauty and outrageousness, in the graciousness of the heart." Kindness is one characteristic of spiritual maturity. It begins with kindness toward the self. When we know ourselves with compassion, we can then be kind to others. Patience is another characteristic. Impatience comes from trying to control or push, while patience comes from having a trust in life. Another is immediacy, the ability to be fully present in each moment with ourselves and with others. A related trait is flexibility. Kornfield says, "Spiritual maturity allows us, like bamboo, to move in the wind, to respond to the world with our understanding and our hearts, to respect the changing circumstances around us. The spiritually mature person has learned the great arts of staying present and letting go." Other qualities Kornfield equates with spiritual maturity include non-idealism, or letting go of notions of perfectionism in yourself or others; having an integrated spiritual practice that is expressed in your life; questioning, rather than blindly accepting authority; the ability to embrace and hold opposites; accepting ordinariness rather than seeking mystical states; and finally, living in relationship to all things.

It is not necessary to label yourself Christian,

Jew, Buddhist, Wiccan, or Muslim. All spiritual teachings serve to remind you of who you really are. They aspire to awaken the qualities of your essential nature: love, compassion, joy, acceptance, and inner peace. The only practice you need is to quiet your mind, open your heart, begin to see more clearly the nature of reality and truth, and then strive to live it. As you move into authentic relationship with yourself and others, you can't help but awaken the good for all people. That's all there really is.

# TWELVE

# Coming Home

*Unmoored, unmated, ungrounded;*
*situated squarely in that terrifying paradise called freedom,*
*precipitously out on so many emotional limbs,*
*as if I had just been born; and in fact,*
*I was being reborn as the woman I was to become.*

—Alice Walker
*The Way Forward is With a Broken Heart*

H ave you noticed how the spiritual path is often
linked with images of coming home? And that it
is typically the male who leaves his physical home
and ventures out into the world to embark on a spiritual quest, sometimes called the hero's journey? And

if he returns home, it is after having gained something precious for himself, and he is more valued by his community? A classic is the story of Buddha, the Prince Siddhartha, who was called to leave his family and privileged life in order to realize his true nature, to become enlightened, and become a great teacher. In many ways, the Buddha's journey was a response to the same psycho-spiritual issues so many contemporary women face today at midlife, specifically enmeshment in societal roles and expectations that limit her spiritual growth. The women's stories in this book are about leaving home to come home to her authentic self.

Coming home to her true self is a stage of women's midlife development that isn't yet named. It is frowned upon in many cultures because it locates the source of freedom within each woman herself, rather than in an external authority. It is through many symbolic acts of self-creation, risk, and choice that a woman connects with her inner spiritual home. Women who travel this path universally feel alone and deeply conflicted because it is indeed a solo journey, one that usually must be undertaken outside the confines of her ordinary life. It always entails some sort of withdrawal from the familiar—either physically or metaphorically—while an essential inner transition takes place. Following is an excerpt from my leaving home Journal.

*What was calling me? Home. I didn't understand
what that was, except as a subtle yearning that lived just
beneath the alienation that blanketed my soul. This alienation was caused by my inability to be authentic in my
relationship to myself and others, by numbing my feelings
in my love relationship. My spirit had been deadened by
the emotional abuse I lived with, by putting myself in a
box and choosing to live in neutral rather than leave
home. Lacking a way to renew myself, the demands of
my profession further drained my life energy, and I had no
emotional resiliency left. I was afraid I was dying! Even
as a doctoral level psychologist, I didn't trust I would be
okay if I left home. Then grace intervened, and I gave
myself freedom by striking out alone, taking refuge within
myself, and trusting that whatever I needed would show
up. And it did. I found clarity by embracing both the dark
and the light. I began to integrate the fragmented parts of
myself and embarked on an authentic life that wasn't possible when I was so alienated, so fragmented that I simply
could not see in the dark. I couldn't hear what was calling
me until I took the leap into the unknown, entered the
emptiness, and found true home within.*

In the spiritual sense, home is your inner place
of spiritual nourishment, the locus of your authentic
self, your essence. On the other hand, home is also
an invention, an idea. For most people, the word
home represents their connection to what is most
basic and essential: feelings of belonging, safety,

warmth. This sense of home as refuge is probably as old as the human need for shelter. In the best of all worlds, home is the name we give to the first place where we feel safely held, loved, and connected. It is our foundation for personal value and belonging, and from here the personality is shaped. For those who have not had a positive experience of home, there can be deep absence and loneliness associated with home. For many midlife women who have been keepers of hearth and hearts, and whose biological and social roles revolved around others, the idea of home can also be fraught with ambivalent feelings.

Each of us has a view of reality that is derived largely from our early experience of family and social relationships . . . from our initial home. We remain stuck in our personal view of reality until we can make the choice to break free and find our true home. Kayla discovered later in life that the call to come home is bound up in choice. She related a painful history, embedded in her lonely Jewish childhood and marriage, of being a pleaser. After years as an unhappy victim, she realized she had choices. When she decided to risk choosing truth over her fear of being unloved and alone, she blossomed. Kayla said, "I found I can be truthful without blaming or judging the other. When I ceased blaming I became less judgmental of myself. I now speak my truth with compassion. What others say or do has nothing to do with who I am in my essence. An address no longer defines me. I am at home anywhere with whatever shows up. Home is now that place of nourishment, of rest, where I can be my essential self. I've come full circle, back around to the essential nature with which I was born."

Babies embody pure essence from birth. As babies we are not capable of being aware of our essence, we just *are* essence. We spontaneously express joy, outrage, needs and wants as the moment dictates. As consciousness develops a personality is formed, and in that process we lose touch with our essential nature. We come to believe we are the face we present to the world to keep us safe and invulnerable. The culture we live in reinforces this process by offering unlimited external ways to remain unconscious: over-eating, over-spending, over-working, or busily devoting ourselves to others to the exclusion of recognizing our own deepest needs. We build our lives around trying to fill the emptiness.

There are two kinds of emptiness. The first has an edge to it and feels like a hole that we may spend our life trying to fill. This is the emptiness of something lacking, of that "something more" that is so difficult to define. For instance, if you didn't feel loved as a child or were abused or abandoned at a young age, there can be a deep-seated belief that you are somehow not okay or are lacking in value, and you may live your life accordingly. As an adult, however, you possess the capacity for more mature self-reflection. Through spiritual work and the tools provided throughout this book, you can bring to light and let go of limiting behaviors and beliefs about yourself, and realize the truth of who you are—and that there really isn't anything missing. Ultimately, it is through realizing and coming home to your true self that the emptiness is filled.

The other kind of emptiness is really spaciousness. It is who we are when we let go of our story and the struggle we repeat endlessly. In Buddhist philosophy this struggle is called *turning on the wheel of samsara*. True freedom is gained by letting go of the endless repetition of your story and getting off the wheel of *samsara*. Any spiritual practice that brings stillness is invaluable for observing how your mind works to keep you stuck in conditioned thinking, and for seeing how you keep yourself turning on the wheel of *samsara*. What is required is to stop and pay attention. Let yourself embrace the emptiness that is your disconnection from true self. In this way you can begin to recover, gradually and with practice, your essential nature.

Authentic self *is* your essential nature. On the most mundane level, *essential* means something you can't live without. The term *essential nature* is an attempt to name the unnameable. John Welwood, in

*Toward a Psychology of Awakening,* describes our essential nature as ". . . a presence that we can directly experience but cannot capture in words, any more than we can really describe what a peach tastes like." While it is indeed difficult to describe in words, essential nature does express itself as a particular set of human qualities that are never lost or damaged, nor do you need to earn them. They are part of your inborn nature and they belong absolutely to you. These qualities are compassion, stillness, joy, inner peace, and personal power.

## QUALITIES OF ESSENCE

COMPASSION ∽ The work of feeling (instead of filling) your inner emptiness requires self-compassion. Compassion is the starting point for your heart opening to your true self, just as you would open to a newborn baby. Women typically find it easier to feel compassion for others then for themselves. Retrieving the heart quality of compassion happens gradually as you pay attention to all of life, within and without. As compassion for self and others deepens, you will find yourself becoming peaceful and still within. This inner stillness is the place from which essential nature arises. It is the source of your longing to come home to the beginning place, to your true self. You may want to review chapter 5 for a more in-depth look at the essential quality of compassion.

STILLNESS ⁓ Kayla discovered that for her, stillness is the key to the door called home. She said, "Only stillness can open me to the spaciousness within myself. Stillness asks what's there? It's the act of paying attention that takes me home. In stillness lies the potential for the rest of my life, for choice. I can choose how I react to outer events—whether this be stress, pain or loneliness—when I bring stillness to the moment. I am now alone in my life, and that's okay because I know that true home lies within me, it is now, and it goes with me always."

In *Stillness Speaks*, Eckhart Tolle distinguishes between stillness and silence. He says, "Silence is helpful, but you don't need it in order to find stillness. Even when there is noise you can be aware of the stillness underneath the noise, of the space in which the noise arises." How is it that external noise can be as helpful as silence? By dropping your resistance to and accepting what is there, you gain an inner peace that is alive within you. Tolle writes, "You find peace not by rearranging the circumstances of your life, but by realizing who you are at the deepest level."

JOY ⁓ Joy is the quality of essence that arises when you connect with whatever you love that is meaningful to you. It could be nature, a garden, a beloved child, or your true self. Joy is your birthright. It is not a momentary happiness like a compliment, or a present, or buying a new car, or having an exciting experience. Rather, joy is the feeling of aliveness that bubbles just beneath all of your ups and downs. It is found when you are truly present with the moment, appreciating it for what it is. It is knowing who you are at the deepest level. Joy is found in simple things—acts of kindness, the love of parent for child, finding pleasure in the happiness of others. It deepens our understanding, brings inner peace, gratitude, compassion, and a respect for life. Often when a woman contacts the emptiness within, it is easier for her to feel sadness and grief. For men, it is easier to feel anger. By bringing awareness and acceptance to the grief, sadness or anger, the essential quality of joy can emerge.

Jacquie, whom you met in chapter 1, generously shared her current thoughts about coming home. She said, "An address was important when my children were growing up. Back then it was OUR home—filled with laughter and tears; silly and serious moments; favorite casseroles, apple pie, homemade bread. Homework, girlfriends, boyfriends, best friends. Celebrations, graduations, birthdays and holidays. Love was poured in and poured out. Growth happened and all too soon OUR home became an empty nest. As I spiraled into midlife, my sense of home changed in profound ways. Home is no longer a matter of address or place.

"Today my home is the cliff I stand on as I watch the ocean waves crash to shore; the warm beach sand covering my toes; a cave hidden at high tide—dark, damp, quiet, holding eternity for me. My home is Mother Earth, her rich damp soil nourishing her fields of wild flowers. Her forests of redwood, oak and willow create homes for me and a myriad of creatures to share. Homes within homes. Today I share my home with the deer, the hawk and raven, the snake and slug. Today my home includes the moon and stars, the stream, river and ocean. Today my home is where my heart sings, where I find pleasure and beauty, wherever my spirit is present. My home is a haven, a reflection, a sacred space, a simple place of rest and nourishment." Like so many midlife women, Jacquie connects with her essence through nature. Her sense of home now embodies the essential qualities of joy and inner peace.

PEACE ∞ Peace is a sense of innate well-being that is available to each of us when we release, forgive, and accept. Much like sadness and joy, peace and power are two dimensions of the same essential quality. How do you find these essential qualities? The doorway is inner stillness. What opens this door? All you need to do is to stop and enter the stillness within. This can be frightening at first because letting go of the false self is a kind of death. Your ego may experience terror, anxiety and contraction. Further, you may have the idea that stillness or silence are nothingness. This is not true. Next time silence engulfs you, just listen to it. You will notice it has its own nameless sound, depth and taste. It is not just the absence of noise and thought. There is a primal intelligence about silence. The twin sister of outer silence is inner stillness. Listening to silence is a spiritual practice. As you pay attention to the silence around you, you are not thinking, your noisy thoughts are absent, yet you are aware. You are still. It is this inner stillness that gives birth to the essential quality of inner peace.

Symptoms of inner peace include letting go of judging yourself and others. There may be a loss of interest in conflict, in worrying about the actions of others and other things you can't change. There is an ability to enjoy every moment, accompanied by frequent episodes of appreciation and connectedness with others and with nature. There is a tendency to let things happen, instead of using control to make them happen according to your wishes. You may enjoy thinking and acting spontaneously, rather than from fears rooted in past experiences. There may even be frequent attacks of smiling, loving others, and letting yourself be loved.

PERSONAL POWER ∾ Peace is often misunderstood, but power is even more misunderstood. Power is usually equated with people, institutions, nations, and corporations getting what they want. Having power *over* is false power and is familiar to most of us from childhood and the work world. Personal power, however, is located within you. It is intrinsic to essence. It is the inner power that allows you to be vulnerable, to be present with what is, because it knows that who you are cannot be destroyed. False power destroys people and things. Real power destroys the false beliefs we hold about ourselves, illuminates the truth of who we are, and transcends the tyranny of the mind. Real power is personal. It dwells in the stillness of peace and presence.

Women have been afraid of their personal power because letting ourselves be seen and heard entails risk of losing love and connection. So we have difficulty seeing what is real in us. We are relational beings—our female soul will always struggle with how to be with another and also be connected with our self. The ultimate power is the power to BE. There is always some tension between what is true and not true. If you bring your awareness to this tension, you'll notice it gets stronger and more insistent. If you really pay attention, you will hear the voice of authenticity. The call compels the answer. When you answer the call, you can trust it will bring you home.

In Western culture, spirituality seems to have acquired a bad name. This is partly because of the tendency in our culture to idealize spiritual teachers.

In doing so we give them too much authority, and power that is frequently abused. There is a long line of spiritual teachers who have come to the West to teach over the last thirty years, only to succumb to the false power young American spiritual seekers have bestowed upon them. These young Americans were disenchanted with our materialistic society and looked to spiritual fulfillment and conscious community as a way to fill their emptiness. Many experienced a sense of coming home when they found a spiritual teacher who, like a good father or mother, loved and cared for them. They felt safely held and easily merged with and idealized the spiritual teacher. Often the teacher or mentor is unaware of his or her own need to be adored and idealized, and succumbs to the emotional needs of the devoted students. To learn more about the problem of how we idealize our spiritual teachers and communities, I recommend Stephen Cope's *Yoga and the Quest for the True Self*.

It is easy to confuse spiritual teachers with power when we project our own personal power onto teachers and, as a result, do not see them (or ourselves) very clearly. One such example from my personal experience is the travesty that happened at Kripalu Center for Yoga and Health, where I once lived as a spiritual life trainee. Whenever I walked through the doors of the Kripalu ashram I felt wrapped in the warm blanket of belonging. Each night I would attend *satsang*, which is an evening of chanting and dancing, followed by a talk on spiritual matters by Kripalu's founder and guru, Amrit Desai, whom we called Gurudev (beloved teacher). I was a bit older than most of the residents at that time, and I spent much of these *satsang* evenings curiously watching the young American residents' adoration of the guru. I wondered about the looks of adulation, and the frenzy of sensual dancing that accelerated along with the music, drumming, and chanting. The young women appeared at times to become orgasmic. Gurudev was indeed a sensual man—tall, slender, with exotic East Indian features, shoulder length hair, and long white and gold robes. At the same time there were rumors that Gurudev was sexually involved with his female assistant, who wore flowing robes similar to his, traveled with him, and demonstrated utter adoration of him during the many religious ceremonies in which I participated. I have never been a guru worshiper, yet I refused to believe these rumors. But later there were accusations from other women of sexual transgressions. A few years after I left Kripalu, Amrit Desai was banished from the spiritual community he founded, and he left in his wake hundreds of disillusioned "children" who were required to grow up and claim their own spiritual authority. And the community was required to move onto the next stage of growth and maturity—which it has done beautifully.

If you decide to pursue a spiritual teacher, be aware of the human tendency to project your longings for love and recognition and mistake them for buried longings for home. Be careful not to project false power onto an authority figure in exchange for the illusion of being safely held, loved, and wrapped in the warm blanket of belonging. The only thing you can come home to is your true self. Nobody can give that to you because you already have it. Find a teacher who will relate to your Beingness, who can help you see your false self and bring your lost and neglected parts under one roof, and who will bring truth and compassion to all interactions, enabling your essential nature to awaken.

This life is a journey of awakening. As with any journey, it doesn't happen all at once. It takes a long time and, like the Velveteen Rabbit, you can be pretty well worn by the time you become real. Once you heed the call to awaken, you will face challenging choices and changes. As the call becomes more insistent you are asked to pay attention, to embrace stillness, and listen deeply to the voice of true home. Do not seek truth outside yourself. Dig deep to unravel the mystery of your Being. There is no road map, for this is a solo journey best accomplished with trust, love and support from those who understand, and with courage to shine your light into shadow places. Do not be afraid. The only demon is your small self. You may encounter stigma from those who want you to stay in your small self. If so, ask yourself, "What is the price, what are the rewards?" Many women stay right where they are in real life and relationships and still answer the call to awaken. Others must strike out alone as they undertake the journey. Either route can take you Home. Which path awaits you? It is my hope that the personal stories, so generously shared in this book by courageous women, will light your way.

> *The time will come*
> *when, with elation,*
> *you will greet yourself arriving*
> *at your own door, in your own mirror,*
> *and each will smile at the other's welcome,*
> *and say, sit here. Eat.*
> *You will love again the stranger who was your self.*
> *Give wine. Give bread. Give back your heart*
> *to itself, to the stranger who has loved you*
> *all your life, whom you ignored*
> *for another, who knows you by heart.*
> *Take down the love letters from the bookshelf,*
> *the photographs, the desperate notes,*
> *peel your own image from the mirror.*
> *Sit. Feast on your life.*
>
> —Derek Walcott
> "Love After Love"

# RESOURCES and REFERENCES

Aburdene, P. and J. Naisbitt. 1992. *Megatrends for women*. NY: Villard Books.

Alter, W. 1995. "The yang heart of yin: On women's spiritual nature." *The Quest* Winter: 41-45.

Artress, L. 1995. *Walking a sacred path: Rediscovering the labyrinth as a spiritual tool*. NY: Riverhead.

Ban Breathnach, S. 1998. *Something more: Excavating your authentic self*. NY: Warner Books.

Borysenko, J. 1996. *A woman's book of life*. NY: Riverhead.

Bridges, W. 2004. *Transitions: Making sense of life's changes*. 25th ed. NY: Da Capo Press.

Brown, D. 2003. *The da Vinci code*. NY: Doubleday.

Burch, M. 1995. *Simplicity*. BC, Canada: New Society Publishers.

Campbell, J. 2008. *Hero with a thousand faces*. 3rd ed. NY: New World Library.

Chinen, A. 1996. *Waking the world: Classic tales of women and the heroic feminine*. NY: Tarcher.

Chodron, P. 2001. *The places that scare you*. Boston: Shambhala.

Collins, G. 2003. *America's women*. NY: William Morrow.

Cope, S. 1999. *Yoga and the quest for the true self*. NY: Bantam.

Daly, Mary. 1995. In *Midlife meditations for women*,

edited by M. Brady. NY: HarperOne.

Fishman, B. 2002. *Emotional healing through mindfulness meditation.* VT: Inner Traditions.

Gadon, Elinor. 1995. *The once and future goddess.* NY: Harper & Row.

Gimbutas, Marija. 1982. *Goddesses and gods of old Europe.* Berkeley: University of California Press.

Gunther, B. 1983. *Energy, ecstacy and your seven vital chakras.* CA: Newcastle Publishing.

Houston, S. 2006. *Invoking Mary Magdalene: Accessing the wisdom of the divine feminine.* Boulder, CO: Sounds True, Inc.

Huber, C. 1998. *The Key.* CA: Keep It Simple Books.

Jack, Dana C. 1993. *Silencing the self: Women and depression.* Cambridge: Harvard University Press.

Keen, S. 1991. *Fire in the belly: On being a man.* NY: Bantam.

Kornfield, J. 1993. *A path with heart: A guide through the perils and promises of spiritual life.* NY: Bantam.

Kundtz, D. 1998. *Stopping: How to be still when you have to keep going.* San Francisco: Conari Press.

Leider, R. and D. Shapiro. 1995. *Repacking your bags.* San Francisco: Berrett-Koehler.

Mountain Dreamer, O. 1999. *The Invitation.* NY: HarperOne.

Nelson, M. 1993. *Coming home: The return to true self.* CA: Nataraj Publishing.

Nelson, M. 2001. "Self-compassion as a characteristic of spirituality" in *Self-compassion: Secret to spiritual success*. www.learningplaceonline.com

Northrup, C. 2006. *The wisdom of menopause*. 2nd ed. NY: Bantam Books.

Pressman, K. 1992. *The big picture book: A primer of spiritual qualities for adults*. Boulder, CO: Jester Press.

Ray, P. and S. Anderson. 2000. *The cultural creatives*. NY: Harmony Books.

Richardson, C. 2004. "Topic of the week: Forgiveness." *Life Makeover E-newsletter*.

Rilke, R. M., A. Barrows, and J. Macy. 2005. *In praise of mortality: Selections from Rilke's duino elegies and sonnets to Orpheus*. NY: Riverhead.

Ruether, R. 1995. "Ecofeminism" in *Ecofeminism and the sacred*, edited by Carol Adams. NY: Continuum Publishing.

Roszak, T., M. Gomes, and A. Kanner. 1995. *Ecopsychology: Restoring the earth, healing the mind*. San Francisco: Sierra Club Books.

Robin, V. and Dominguez, J. 1993. *Your money or your life*. NY: Penguin.

Schachter-Shalomi, Z. and Miller, R. 1995. *From age-ing to sage-ing: A profound new vision of growing older*. NY: Warner Books.

Spretnak, C. (Ed.).1982. *Politics of women's spirituality*. NY: Anchor Press.

Starhawk. 1999. *The spiral dance: A rebirth of ancient religions.* NY: HarperOne.

Threshold quotes from *Parabola*. Spring 2000.

Tolle, E. 2003. *Stillness Speaks.* Vancouver: Namaste Publishing/CA: New World Library.

Trungpa, Chogyam. 1984. *Shambhala: The sacred path of the warrior.* Boston: Shambhala.

Walcott, D. *Collected Poems 1948-1984.* NY: Farrar, Straus & Giroux, LLC.

Walker, A. 2001. *The way forward is with a broken heart.* NY: Ballantine.

Walker, C. "Psychologist finds self-compassion helps people cope with failure" in WFU News, Wake Forest University News Service, August 22, 2005.

Welwood, J. 2000. *Toward a psychology of awakening: Buddhism, psychotherapy, and the path of personal and spiritual transformation.* Boston: Shambhala.

## ORDER INFORMATION

*Endings. Beginnings . . .*
*When Midlife Women Leave Home in Search of Authenticity*


❖ Send a check for $20 plus $3 shipping within the U.S. to:

BeMe Press
1081 Artemis Circle
Lafayette, CO 80026

❖ Order using PayPal at www.BeMePress.com

❖ Order online at www.Amazon.com

LaVergne, TN USA
02 July 2010
188080LV00001B/5/P